Word-of-Mouth Advertising

Online and Off

How to Spark Buzz, Excitement, and Free Publicity for Your Business or Organization

With Little or No Money

By Lynn Thorne

WORD-OF-MOUTH ADVERTISING ONLINE AND OFF: HOW TO SPARK BUZZ, EXCITEMENT, AND FREE PUBLICITY FOR YOUR BUSINESS OR ORGANIZATION — WITH LITTLE OR NO MONEY

ISBN-13: 978-1-60138-011-1   ISBN-10: 1-60138-011-9

Library of Congress Cataloging-in-Publication Data

Thorne, Lynn, 1967-
  Word-of-mouth advertising online and off : how to spark buzz, excitement, and free publicity for your business or organization with little or no money / by Lynn Thorne.
     p. cm.
  Includes bibliographical references and index.
  ISBN-13: 978-1-60138-011-1 (alk. paper)
  ISBN-10: 1-60138-011-9 (alk. paper)
  1. Word-of-mouth advertising. 2. Viral marketing. 3. Internet advertising. I. Title.

  HF5827.95.T46 2008
  659.13'3--dc22
                              2008005880

COVER & INTERIOR LAYOUT DESIGN: Vickie Taylor • vtaylor@atlantic-pub.com

Printed in the United States

Printed on Recycled Paper

DEDICATION

For my leading men — Mike, Zach, and Corey

Also for Mom and Dad — you inspire me.

We recently lost our beloved pet "Bear," who was not only our best and dearest friend but also the "Vice President of Sunshine" here at Atlantic Publishing. He did not receive a salary but worked tirelessly 24 hours a day to please his parents. Bear was a rescue dog that turned around and showered myself, my wife Sherri, his grandparents Jean, Bob, and Nancy and every person and animal he met (maybe not rabbits) with friendship and love. He made a lot of people smile every day.

We wanted you to know that a portion of the profits of this book will be donated to The Humane Society of the United States.

–Douglas & Sherri Brown

THE HUMANE SOCIETY
OF THE UNITED STATES ©

The human-animal bond is as old as human history. We cherish our animal companions for their unconditional affection and acceptance. We feel a thrill when we glimpse wild creatures in their natural habitat or in our own backyard.

Unfortunately, the human-animal bond has at times been weakened. Humans have exploited some animal species to the point of extinction.

The Humane Society of the United States makes a difference in the lives of animals here at home and worldwide. The HSUS is dedicated to creating a world where our relationship with animals is guided by compassion. We seek a truly humane society in which animals are respected for their intrinsic value, and where the human-animal bond is strong.

Want to help animals? We have plenty of suggestions. Adopt a pet from a local shelter, join The Humane Society and be a part of our work to help companion animals and wildlife. You will be funding our educational, legislative, investigative, and outreach projects in the U.S. and across the globe.

Or perhaps you'd like to make a memorial donation in honor of a pet, friend, or relative? You can through our Kindred Spirits program. And if you'd like to contribute in a more structured way, our Planned Giving Office has suggestions about estate planning, annuities, and even gifts of stock that avoid capital gains taxes.

Maybe you have land that you would like to preserve as a lasting habitat for wildlife. Our Wildlife Land Trust can help you. Perhaps the land you want to share is a backyard — that's enough. Our Urban Wildlife Sanctuary Program will show you how to create a habitat for your wild neighbors.

So you see, it's easy to help animals. And The HSUS is here to help.

The Humane Society of the United States
2100 L Street NW
Washington, DC 20037
202-452-1100
www.hsus.org

Table of Contents

Dedication 3

Introduction 13

Chapter 1: First Words 19

What Is Word of Mouth? 20

What Is Word-of-Mouth Marketing? 21

Advantage 1: Trust 25

Advantage 2: Efficiency 25

Advantage 3: Cost 25

Advantage 4: Language Barriers 26

Advantage 5: An Edge 26

Organic versus Amplified 27

Oldies but Not-So Goodies 29

Five Steps to Ultimate Marketing Buzz 34

Step One 34

Step Two 36

Step Three.. 37

Step Four 41

Step Five 42

Benefits of Word of Mouth 43

What's the Buzz? 45

A Word About Ethics.. 46

After-Word 47

Chapter 2: The C-Word...........49

Care and Feeding of Your Customer.......................... 50

The Customer-Generated Sales Force 59

Building Your Sales Force 61

Microsharing... 65

Community Marketing 66

The Customer Evangelist 67

Loyalty Programs.. 70

Developing a Loyalty Program............................... 72

Your Other Loyal Sales Force................................. 74

Networking.. 75

After-Word 80

Chapter 3: The B-Word 83

Buzzing.. 84

Creating Buzz Among Customers............................. 84

Hook 'Em 84

Call to Action 86

Maximize Your Resources 88

Create a Theme 90

Top Mistakes in Creating Buzz 91

Live Buzz Marketing 92

Keeping the Buzz Buzzing 95

Event Marketing 98

How to Track the B-uzz 101

Checklist 106

After-Word 107

Chapter 4: Virtual Words 109

World Wide Web of Mouth 110

Internet Marketing 110

Get a Good Domain Name 112

Build Your Web Site, and They Will Come 112

Size Sometimes Matters 113

Optimize Your Site for Search Engines 114

Plant the Seeds 115

Geotargeting Is Not Just for Rock Hunters 115

Make Your Landing Pages User-Friendly 116

Goldilocks Was Here 116

Let the Consumer Do the Work 116

Online Press Releases 119

Discussion Forums and Boards 121

Affiliate Marketing 123

After-Word 124

Chapter 5: All The World's a Stage 127

Developing a Campaign 128

Craft Your Message 129

Target Your Talkers 131

Listen Up 134

Haven't You Heard? 136

Tracking Devices 145

After-Word 145

Chapter 6: For-Words 147

Viral Marketing 148

Viral Videos 149

Key Elements 151

After-Word 158

Chapter 7: Is That Even a Word? 161

Blog Marketing 162

Creating a Blog 165

What Should You Blog About? 166

Promoting Your Blog 170

Blog Advertising 172

After-Word 174

Chapter 8: In Words & Out Words... 177

E-mail Marketing.. 178

'Tis the Season for E-mails..................................... 179

Make It Count 181

E-mail Newsletters 184

Generating Lists 186

Legal-ese... 188

A Word of Warning.. 189

After-Word 190

Chapter 9: A Word From Our Sponsors.. 193

Nonprofit Word-of-Mouth Marketing..................... 194

Blogs — Again 195

Virtual Worlds 197

Viral Marketing.. 199

Social Networking 199

Widgets 204

Podcasting.. 205

Publicity Stunts 209

Cause Marketing... 211

The Effect of Spokespeople.................................... 214

How to Build and Maintain a Reputation 215

Fundraiser Letters 215

Testimonials 216

Online Reputation Management 217

Crisis Management 218

After-Word 220

Chapter 10: The F-Word 223

Keeping It Real 224

Word of Mouth Marketing Association Toolkit 225

Honesty of Relationship 226

Honesty of Opinion 226

Honesty of Identity 226

Taking Responsibility 227

Respecting the Rules 227

When Hiring an Agency 228

Effects of Unethical Campaigns 229

A Word About Agents 232

Blogola 235

After-Word 236

Chapter 11: Bad Words 239

Sometimes Bad Press Happens 239

Managing Negative Buzz 241

What Are They Saying? 242

Responding to Bad Press 243

Promote Yourself.. 246

Turn a Negative Into a Positive 247

After-Word 250

Conclusion: Famous Last Words 253

Appendix A: Proven Secrets & Tips for WOMM 255

Appendix B: More Types of Low-Cost (or Free!) WOMM Campaigns 259

About the Author 273

Glossary 275

Index 281

INTRODUCTION

TESTIMONIALS. Just the word alone conjures up thoughts of the slightly odd and overly enthusiastic in-a-creepy-sort-of-way youth minister at a Southern Baptist church I met while I was growing up. His name was David, and he said we needed to give our testimony to anyone and everyone. David stood behind the philosophy that we could convert the entire planet to Christianity simply by telling each person we saw about our faith and our daily walk with the Lord. Now, you may be different, but when someone stops me in a shopping center parking lot and starts preaching, I walk away. Quickly. I never did understand how he thought that cornering unsuspecting strangers with our personal story of salvation could work. I still think he was more than a little bit nuts. However, after years of being brow-beaten by ads, commercials, and other marketing tactics, I finally have to admit that maybe he was on to something. It hearkens back to the whole zealot thing. Religion aside, real people are the most convincing advertisements there are. If cousin Carrie has something really good to share, she just has to tell people about it because she is so excited about it, and because she thinks they can benefit from it. Also, her intense passion about it will make people want to listen.

What will not make people pay attention is yet another 30-second commercial or a half-page ad. After all, the public is inundated with messages as soon as the alarm goes off in the morning. David Shenk (a different David than the guy I knew, and one who actually has a working brain), who wrote Data Smog, says the average person is bombarded by 3,000 advertising messages a day, with every billboard, newspaper, magazine, and TV screaming at you to buy this product or that service. You are exposed to so many of them you tune them out. You question why you should listen to them. After all, you are likely to see the same ad for the same product, or a supposedly even better one, in the next metro station, the next newspaper, or the next commercial break. Furthermore, it is highly unlikely that you will pay any more attention to that one.

But what if your best friend tells you, "I found the most amazing product. It actually gets my kids' crayon marks off the wall." You would probably listen even if you do not have cute little rascals who act like Matisse with Crayolas because the endorsement came from a trusted source. Someone who is not affiliated with the Miracle-Crayon-Remover-Doohickey recommended it and that makes your ears more apt to perk up. You consider whether it might remove the scuff marks your spouse left on the wall when he tried to move the dining room chairs — which you told him were too big — through the hallway and into the basement. Your friend tried it with success. Now that you have the endorsement, you want to see for yourself.

Recommendations, product endorsements, testimonials. Call them what you will; getting people to pay attention to marketing simply requires the right delivery method. People are jaded. They have seen and heard too many Ginsu knife-type commercials ("and that's not all! It slices, it dices! Order now!"). The new thing is always bigger and better than the last, except that the last new thing was the cat's meow compared to what came before it. People do not believe the advertising hype because they know better. They are too smart.

What do people believe? Friends and family. Trusted sources. Opinions from others who have no connection to a company. People will listen to people who are not trying to sell them something, but who seem genuinely interested in a product or service. Those people are golden because they are sharing word of mouth and they are the most powerful marketing tool you will never see in a Craftsman tool kit.

So good old David, the youth minister from hell, might have actually known a little about what he was doing. He realized that telling someone — that oh-so-personal form of communication — about something that is helpful, or valuable, or cute, works. I have no way of knowing how many people he actually converted, but he spread his message. And it did not cost him a dime.

The point is, people are more likely to listen to someone they know or someone they trust. In addition, when they discover that the product really does work, or the service really is top-notch, they tell someone else, and word spreads at a fast and furious pace. When a company finds a way to get those people connected more quickly and efficiently, that is the basis of word-of-mouth marketing. That is how, and why, it works. Now all you need to do is create your own Miracle-Crayon-Remover, and start sharing it with strangers in a parking lot. Just watch out for cars backing up.

Word-of-mouth marketing is effective because it makes companies responsible for generating publicity about something, but it puts people in the driver's seat. People listen to people, not ads. They share things they like — or do not — with others.

They do it because they want to help. A 2007 study in Bazaarvoice conducted by Keller Fay Group says customers generally had good intentions when writing reviews. Nearly 80 percent wrote their reviews to reward a company. So, if people are willing to do the marketing for you, and others are willing to listen to them, there must be something to this word-of-mouth-marketing thing.

That is not to say it is a slam dunk. There are word-of-mouth-marketing campaigns that fail, mostly due to poor messaging, poor methods, or poor results tracking. After all, if people cannot understand the message they are supposed to share, the effectiveness of the message gets lost in translation.

So, the secret to a great word-of-mouth campaign is this: develop a great product or service, and get a few people talking about it. Then give them a mouthpiece from which to spread the information far and wide. Listen to what the reaction is, finesse any areas that need to be addressed, and watch your business grow like the proverbial beanstalk. While others are flushing big advertising dollars down the tube, you will be sitting pretty with a great marketing campaign that costs you next to nothing, but has your business being talked about from here to Siam.

Oh, and by the way, the "best friend" in the above-mentioned tale was me. I fell in love with the Mister Clean Magic Eraser after it removed some folk-art renditions of Rudolph that my son made on our kitchen wall. I told everyone I know about my new favorite product. I'm not sure, but I think Procter & Gamble's stock tripled that year. So, here I am again, spreading the message on to you. I assure you, I am in no way affiliated with or married to Mr. Clean. But if P&G wants to give me a lifetime supply of Magic Erasers or even send the real Mr. Clean to be my live-in housekeeper for mentioning them in this book, I can live with that.

First Words

WHICH came first, the customer or the marketer? Without a customer, the marketer had no one to pitch to. But without a marketer, the customer had no one hyping up a product. Fortunately, there is no need to ponder this question for long because the answer has recently changed thanks to the explosive growth of word-of-mouth marketing.

In this brave new marketing world, consumers have become the marketers. They no longer just buy the product, they sell it by talking about it. Suddenly the customer has become far more powerful than ever before. And the marketer has a whole different role.

Lest we forget, the public is also smarter than ever. People refuse to be sold to. They resist the ads, the marketing hype, and the old-fashioned sales techniques. They know better. They want better. They are demanding better. And they will get it because businesses are taking notice, or they will close their doors.

This chapter explains:

- Word-of-mouth marketing, its advantages, and disadvantages (the latter is a very short section)

- The difference between organic and amplified word of mouth

- Why traditional marketing does not make the grade today

- The five steps to creating word of mouth

- The differences between word of mouth, viral and buzz marketing, and other buzz words

- Why ethics rule in word-of-mouth marketing

WHAT IS WORD OF MOUTH?

My son wants to be a superhero when he grows up. Specifically, he wants to be Wonder Boy, and he wants me to be Wonder Woman. Do not laugh — it is his dream. He is working on his super powers, trying to figure out how to fly and how to see through buildings. (I am just waiting until he is old enough to want to see through women's clothes, but that is a topic for another book.) What he does not know is that he already has amazing strength. He has the power to help make a business succeed or a new toy fail, and he was born with it.

It is called word of mouth. Try not to be jealous of my son — you have the power, too. You have been using it all of your life, and you may not have known it. When you tell a friend about a great movie you just saw, that is word of mouth. When you warn your sister not to eat at that new restaurant in town, that is word of mouth. In addition, when you recommend your favorite babysitter to your new neighbor, that is — you guessed it — word of mouth.

Word of mouth is not science. It is a heck of a lot easier to understand than osmosis, the Bernoulli Principle, or photosynthesis. It is the simple act of telling somebody about something, good or bad. You are sharing your opinion with someone you know. Since that person knows you, he or she is more likely to listen. You are a trusted source. As a result of your suggestion, he or she will likely see that movie next, skip the above-referenced restaurant like it serves hard-boiled baby octopus, or save that babysitter's number in the speed-dial for the next date night. All it took was your word.

The power of word of mouth is infinite. When your friend sees that great movie (while using your terrific babysitter and going to an entirely different restaurant), he or she will tell a few friends, who also make plans to hotfoot it to the theater after booking your own personal Mary Poppins and making reservations at any eatery that does not serve creatures with more than four legs. The cycle escalates until the movie has grossed a bazillion bucks, the octopus restaurant has gone under, and your favorite babysitter is now too busy to watch your kids.

What Is Word-of-Mouth Marketing?

That was word of mouth in a nutshell. Word-of-mouth marketing takes it a little further. It involves learning how to make word of mouth work to fit a marketing objective. It is giving someone a good reason to talk about your business and facilitating a way to make that happen.

What it is not is a fly-by-night phenomenon. It is not a fad. It is not a Pet Rock, a Rubik's Cube, or a mood ring. According to the

Word-of-Mouth Marketing Association, 82 percent of the Inc. 500 is already using word of mouth. These companies did not get where they are by engaging in folly. They are taking it seriously, and so should you.

Word-of-mouth marketing is the most honest form of marketing because consumers are sharing their own opinions, independent of messaging and manipulation. The benefits are not only straightforward — they are downright undeniable. It does not cost a million dollars. It simply takes a good product or service, a company with a clear and concise message, and people willing to talk about it. The influence of word of mouth is undeniably powerful:

- The Travel Industry Association says family and friends are the number one source for information about places to visit or about flights, hotels, and rental cars.

- A Nielson survey found that 78 percent of respondents trusted recommendations from consumers, a total 15 percent higher than the second most credible source (newspapers).

- MTV and Nickelodeon report that 88 percent of teens visit a Web site because a friend sent them the link.

- Maritz Marketing Research reports that 53 percent of moviegoers rely to some extent on a recommendation from someone they know.

- Synovate says 65 percent of blog readers are interested in reading others' opinions.

- On average, one-third of online gamers have doled out vehicle purchase advice and 63 percent of the car talk focused on which make or model to purchase.

- According to eMarketer, 59 percent of college students pick word of mouth as their preferred method for learning about new products and services.

- Consumers prefer peer reviews over expert reviews by a margin of six to one.

- Fifty percent of business executives report they are highly likely to buy a product or service based on word of mouth; 49 percent pass on what they have heard to others.

- A whopping 85 percent of college students primarily learn about new products through word of mouth.

The numbers are only expected to go higher. Research and trend analysis company eMarketer projected that in 2007, 64 million adults shared advice about products and services, and 25 million people exerted influence online. And that is when the technology behind word-of-mouth marketing was still in its infancy. That was no small feat.

In fact, many experts seem to think that broadcasting to the masses is now passé. You will likely hear the phrase a "public of one" more and more often, with the message that marketers need to focus on speaking to individuals. With billions of consumers, how do the "big dogs" market to them individually? Smaller companies have a big advantage here, to be sure, because they are closer to and interact more with their customers. Even the smallest business may have trouble reaching each individual client, though.

That is where word-of-mouth marketing comes in. Give people relevant, meaningful, and entertaining content that compels them to share it with others, and they will help influence your buyers for you, one at a time.

Marketing professionals are paying attention to the message. Spending shows that marketers are aware of, and ready to tap into, the power of word-of-mouth marketing. A PQ Media study showed that corporations spent $1 billion on word of mouth in 2007. Sounds like a lot of money, right? Wait, there is more. Spending on word-of-mouth marketing campaigns is expected to quadruple by 2011.

Despite the statistics, many marketers are reluctant to turn over control — and dollars — to word-of-mouth marketing strategies, mainly because they are fearful. Marketing as an industry has spent decades putting just the right spin on things. To willingly hand over that power to the public is worthy of hesitation, but only for a moment. This book will make it clear why.

With the advent of Web 2.0, word-of-mouth marketing was able to hit its stride. Suddenly consumers were not only spreading the message among themselves, they were creating it through customer-generated marketing (also known as CGM). It took on a proverbial life of its own. Marketers became instantly able to access millions of people the world over in a format of their choosing.

Yet the industry still balks. The 2007 *Media, Myths & Realities* report from Ketchum and the USC Annenberg Strategic Public Relations Center reveals that less than one in four communicators has a word-of-mouth strategy in place. Sure, it is scary when, as a marketing professional, you are putting your carefully crafted message in someone else's hands. At the same time, if more people are willing to listen to that message because it comes from someone they trust instead of a traditional ad, it seems prudent (and downright smart) to stand back and let word of mouth work its magic.

Why not review the advantages and then decide whether it is worth the risk to give up that control.

Advantage 1: Trust

The public implicitly trusts other customers, not marketers. Consumers are growing increasingly skeptical of and bored by traditional marketing methods. They know when they are being "sold" to and most of the time they resist the sale. Yet if another customer says that he or she had great results with a new product, you would be hard pressed to find a more powerful endorsement.

Advantage 2: Efficiency

Advertisers will happily take your money to launch a big, splashy media campaign. The catch is that they cannot necessarily reach your target audience as well as you can. Of course, you personally are not reaching your entire target audience; you will make it your goal to reach a few passionate customers who are in your target group and enable them do a large share of the marketing. Again, they have the implicit trust of their peers as well as much closer (and probably more frequent) access than you could ever hope to achieve with an ad.

Advantage 3: Cost

How much does it cost you when one of your customers says to another prospective client, "Gee, I just tried this new dry cleaners over on 3rd Street. They're terrific. They not only do free pleats but they gave me a sample of a great spot remover when I picked up my clothes." That is priceless advertising right there and it costs you nothing. Need I say more?

Advantage 4: Language Barriers

Consumers speak their own language. They skip the marketing talk like "hand-picked at the peak of perfection" in favor of plain old English. "It works." "You gotta try it." "I love the way it makes my hair feel." Say that in an ad and no one will believe it. Let consumers tell that to their best friend or their coworker and you have a sale. The consumer's voice is powerful and it demands to be heard.

Advantage 5: An Edge

Your competition may not be so savvy. They may not understand the powerful principles behind word-of-mouth marketing. You were smart enough to buy this book, which gives you an edge over your competitors. While they are still doing things the old way, flushing advertising dollars down the proverbial marketing drain, you are creating loyal customers who will sell your business for you.

Is it risky to give up control over your marketing efforts? Sure it is. But after reading the advantages listed above, you have to agree it is a risk that is well worth taking. Besides, you have already bought this book — you may as well put it to good use in your marketing plan.

ORGANIC VERSUS AMPLIFIED

There are two methods of word-of-mouth marketing: one starts with people talking to people and the other begins with a marketer facilitating that discussion. You could call it the difference between C2C and B2C. When someone pipes up at a cocktail party and raves about his or her brand-new dishwasher, that is organic word of mouth. It is also not scintillating party fodder, but that is neither here nor there. When General Electric offers incentives or free samples to help encourage owners of the new Profile to help spread the word about how effective the washer is, that is amplified word of mouth. Both are acceptable, both are real, but both are different in how they start and how far they spread.

In *Creating Customer Evangelists*, Ben McConnell and Jackie Huba write, "people are loyal to people, not necessarily brands." Think about the last time you sought out a direct-sales party to go to at someone's house for jewelry, scrapbooking, skin care, or candles. Most people do not attend home shows because they are dying to add to their own personal collection of any of the above, but they attend and purchase to help a friend or support a loved one. They are loyal, and they spend their money as a result.

Organic word of mouth has been in existence since the Garden of Eden. As long as there is more than one person in a conversation (or if that individual has multiple personalities, I suppose one person is all it takes), there is an opportunity for word of mouth to occur, however benign. That is part of its power — there is little skepticism because the source is up front, honest, and stands to gain nothing by sharing an experience he or she had after trying a product or service. Or an apple, but I digress.

Word of mouth (WOM) is simple. However, many in the marketing world either do not understand its beautiful simplicity, or they are too scared to employ it in their own strategies. The risks of giving up control and putting the message in someone else's hands are certainly there, but they are miniscule compared to the substantial and lucrative rewards awaiting their brand. There is simply no cheaper, or more effective, way to market a product than getting consumers to talk about it.

Need proof? Regardless of whether you liked the movie, *The Blair Witch Project* is a terrific example of how creativity, a few loyal fans, and a forum for them to communicate through beat the pants off Hollywood's practice of spending millions.

In 1999, two students from the University of Central Florida Film School picked up a camcorder and filmed *The Blair Witch Project*, a low-budget indie movie that caught the public totally off guard. The movie itself may not have done much on its own, but Eduardo Sanchez, one of the creators, designed a Web site around the fictitious Blair Witch, a snatcher of unsuspecting kids in Burkittsville, Maryland. Although a complete hoax, the site generated unbelievable buzz, impacting box office sales and eventually grossing the film a cool $250 million worldwide.

It is a fact: people are going to talk. So, if they are going to be talking anyway, you might as well have them talking about your business, and saying good things about it. Word-of-mouth marketing involves creating a community where people can share their opinions, good and bad. It also involves targeting experts or other people who have influence to help spread those opinions, giving them a tool or a voice through which to share them. Finally, it includes tracking the buzz to find out how well it worked.

OLDIES BUT NOT-SO GOODIES

Word of mouth works better than more familiar marketing tactics for several reasons. After all, traditional marketing practices have been around for a while and many of them have made a lasting impact. Images and slogans from years ago ("Which twin has the Toni?" "A little dab'll do ya." or "Where's the beef?") are still quoted today. With messages from Coca-Cola, McDonald's, and Crest seemingly crammed down the public's throat (pun fully intended) at every commercial avenue, marketing seemingly must have everything going for it. But this is not always the case.

Traditional marketing does not cut it anymore. This is the Information Age and messages surround you everywhere you turn. They are on TV, the computer, and the phone. They are in our newspapers, magazines, and emails. While more and more ads are crammed down your throat, the public now has more and more options to ignore them. XM and Sirius satellite radio are commercial free so you can listen to your favorite music and talk shows without being bombarded by yet another jingle. Consumers can escape the never-ending ad stream thanks to TiVo and Replay TV. They can skip commercials by taping their favorite shows on DVDs or VCRs. Most of those products even have a 30-second skip function designed especially to fast-forward past commercials. The public now has several methods at its disposal to escape the endless repetition of product hawking. Technology has done a number on advertisers and it is only likely to become less commercial-friendly. And that is just the first problem with marketing the way it has been done for decades.

Traditional marketing is failing because it is outdated, it is pricey, and it is based on bad business practices. Customers are no longer willing, wanting, or able to be interrupted by commercial messages. Why should they be? While there are more media sources than ever before, the public has grown increasingly skeptical of nearly all media outlets. According to the 2007 Ketchum study *Media, Myths & Realities*, U.S. consumers are less likely than they were in years past to take any information gleaned from media sources at face value. With the exception of cable network news, the public rated all media sources as less credible than in 2006. Even local television news, which was credited with being the most credible, lost ground, dropping from 7.4 in 2006 to 6.9 on a scale of zero to ten.

Consumer confidence is just one reason traditional marketing is giving way to newer forms. There is no question that marketing trends are headed in a whole new direction for good reasons: they simply have to. In the 21st century, there is no room for the old way of doing things. Read on to find out why:

1. It is outdated. College marketing classes teach the four Ps, fundamentals introduced by E. Jerome McCarthy in 1960: product, place, price, and promotion. With all of the changes in the decades since then, including and especially the World Wide Web, it is no surprise that campaigns based on principles introduced when Kennedy was president fail. Granted, the structured world of word-of-mouth marketing is relatively new, but so is teaching up-and-coming Ogilvy wannabes based on products that are out-of-date.

2. Many people mistakenly think marketing and advertising are one and the same, or even worse, they confuse marketing with telemarketing or email marketing. Marketing is the sharing of information about a product or service to get consumers to buy. Tim Cohn's marketing

definition at **www.marketingprinciples.com** has stated it simply yet powerfully: "Marketing is the invisible hand that moves products from sellers to buyers." The American Marketing Association's definition states that "Marketing is the activity, set of institutions, and processes for creating, communicating, delivering, and exchanging offerings that have value for customers, clients, partners, and society at large." There is also MSN Encarta Dictionary's explanation that marketing is "the business activity of presenting products or services to potential customers in such a way as to make them eager to buy," and that it includes "such matters as the pricing and packaging of the product and the creation of demand by advertising and sales campaigns." Do all of those words help you better understand what marketing is? Or did your eyes just glaze over because it was overload? Too many words is rarely a good thing.

Advertising is one slice of the marketing pie, but it should not be the complete strategy. Think about your typical Sunday morning. You are having a cup of coffee while reading the newspaper. How many ads actually entice you to stop reading *The Washington Post* magazine? Or maybe the radio or TV is on in the background. Did you look up long enough to catch the snazzy new ad for toothpaste that prevents cavities while whitening your teeth? Probably not. The same goes for that annoying little card that fell out of the magazine you picked up at your doctor's office. David Shenk, who wrote *Data Smog* (San Francisco: Harper Edge, 1997), claims the average person is exposed to 3,000 advertising messages per day. No wonder most ads get lost in the shuffle. You tune them out — just like those verbose definitions of marketing. You cannot possibly focus on that many messages and have any brain cells left to take to work, balance your checkbook, and walk the dog. So, you ignore them, and every time you do, an advertiser has just thrown time, money, and more importantly, opportunity down the drain.

Take that pop-icon-gone-terribly-wrong Britney Spears, for example. At one time, she was the epitome of what is hot. Everything she touched seemed to hold the promise of multi-million-dollar sales. That is why Pepsi hired her in 2001 to launch one of its most expensive advertising campaigns in history. By 2002, sales had dropped by one percent — kind of like the fizz in your Mountain Dew a day after it was opened.

If marketing is not advertising, it needs to be clearly defined. Ads only tell you about a product or service. Marketing entices you to buy. It convinces you that you cannot live without a said product or service. Marketing is the temptation that makes consumers slide off the fence and into your greener pasture. Advertising may grease the wheels of a sale but marketing closes the door with a resounding, "Thud!"

In the dark days of marketing, it used to be that those with the big bucks wielded the most power. Think of the giants of Madison Avenue — Proctor & Gamble spent $4.51 billion to become the nation's largest advertiser in 2005 according to *Advertising Age*. In the same year, McDonald's paid more than $1.6 billion to convince consumers to visit the Golden Arches. That is a lot of Big Macs and more than a few clogged arteries. That has all changed, though. Not the effect on your cholesterol level, but rather the belief that more money means more power. Think back to *The Blair Witch Project*, which had a production budget of $35,000 and grossed 4,000 times that. It is not always an even payout.

It used to be that marketers expected immediate results and if they did not get them, the campaign was considered a big old failure. The focus is so much on having it all now that you forget the old adage, "Good things come to those who wait." If an ad does not generate million-dollar sales in the first two months, it is considered a flop. However, consider this: Warne, a marketing company based in Toronto, tracked more than 3,500 people who inquired to blue-chip advertisers. Within six months, 19 percent of those inquiring made a purchase. By 25 months, 57 percent had made a purchase. If you only looked at the numbers in the first half of the year, it would not appear that many were sold on the blue-chip boys, but given some time, old Wall Street did all right. Sometimes, it takes people a while to make up their minds. It does not mean a marketing campaign failed — it may just mean it has not yet succeeded.

The final reason that marketing as we know it just cannot survive any more? The cost. Specifically, it is the cost to bring in new accounts. Sure, it is fun to score new customers, but how cost-effective is it? Landing them is expensive, costing between four to six times more than retaining your current clients, depending on whose study you look at. It is cheaper to provide outstanding customer service to keep those who already know—and pay for—your product or service coming back for more. But check the budget of most of the big wigs, and see which line item has more money: marketing or customer service. Go ahead. The book will still be here. Back already? You get the point.

This last reason is so filled with fallacy that it is hard to fathom. (That is a lot of alliteration there, eh? The words just came tripping off the keyboard.) There are award programs for direct marketing agencies that do well with reaching new customers. Everyone celebrates when they land a big new client.

What about the "poor old schmoes" who just diligently keep buying your product? Who throws a party for them? You should, and you should do it visibly and often. We will talk more about serving your current customers in Chapter 2, but in the meantime, your business will benefit more from celebrating them in a big, big way than from throwing money at a traditional ad campaign designed to lure in new clients.

Traditional marketing is not believable. It is not feasible. It is not even smart. Now that you have read each of these reasons individually, it is easy to see why traditional marketing is passé, and why there is room for a new kid in town — specifically, word-of-mouth marketing.

FIVE STEPS TO ULTIMATE MARKETING BUZZ

Like anything, there is a method to the madness of word-of-mouth marketing. It would be terrific if you could just launch a new product and have it fly off the shelves just by sharing it with a few close friends. Unfortunately, it requires a little more work than that. Not a whole lot, mind you — but work nonetheless, along with some proven strategy. Just five basic steps that, when followed correctly, will have the world clamoring for more of your product or service until you cry "Uncle!" or at least, "Sixth-cousin once removed!"

Step One

It is all in who you know. First of all, find the right people. Who needs or wants your product the most? Who is most likely to buy your product or service first? Grab them by the shirttails and hang on like you are a defensive lineman for the Green Bay Packers. You need to know who will be first in line (think of the lines outside Best Buy the morning the X-Box 360 was released) so you will know how to capture their interest. Some people have to be first when it comes to trying something new. Nail them down, and you will be well on your way to buzz heaven.

That is the principle that the magazine *Shock* used when it was preparing to launch its publication. The focus of the rag was to include minimal editorial content, instead focusing on shocking images. Since the readers were also likely to be photojournalists, RepNation Media launched a campaign to not only boost the magazine's awareness and circulation, but also to create more content within the publication.

They used street teams built from their own target readers. In 100 markets nationwide, street teams promoted the magazine with posters, flyers, events, and online networking. The teams were able to communicate with one another through an online portal, sharing pictures of their marketing efforts and tips and ideas with one another to generate a more successful campaign. A Web site was also built and the teams encouraged students to upload their own photos in a competition. Winners won cash and had their pictures published in the magazine.

The Web site received an astounding 16,000 uploaded photos—easily surpassing the original goal of 10,000 pictures by 60 percent. *Shock* even added a college section to its print magazine to feature the top images submitted by students as a result of the successful campaign. By reaching out to the target audience and involving them in the launch, the magazine created better buzz and a built-in readership before the first issue hit the stands.

These human megaphones are known by many names in the industry: influencers, influentials, opinion leaders, connectors, and cheerleaders. Despite the nomenclature, the question is how much power do they actually wield? Can they really convince a 90-year-old great grandma who is hard of hearing to invest in a high-definition LCD flat screen the size of Cincinnati? Probably not. They are not magicians. They probably do not even own a top hat or a magic wand. However, that is not to say that they cannot help your business grow.

They are simply people with loud voices and a large audience, whether on the Web at a social networking site like MySpace or a blog that reaches from here to Brazil. The people you need to know are the people who are eager to try new things and who know a lot of people, whether in real life or cyberland.

Step Two

Massage your message. Once you have found the people most likely to jump on your bandwagon first, develop your message. If you want people to talk, you have to give them something to talk about. You need to craft a very strategic message that is easy to understand and easy to share. Why is your business the best? Why are they wasting their time going anywhere else?

When it prepared to introduce its Fruity Cheerios cereal, General Mills wanted to make sure that its message was clear: Fruity Cheerios is a healthier breakfast cereal that both moms and children can feel good about eating. Eight months before the launch, the company built buzz around the product with a contest in which parents were asked to submit a photo or video of the family enjoying Fruity Cheerios together. Samples were distributed to leading parent bloggers for written reviews, and Web sites with mothers as the primary audience were also given product samples.

The results were sweet, indeed. Internet traffic concerning the cereal increased an average of 250 percent during the eight-month campaign. More importantly, the concept that Fruity Cheerios was a guilt-free food choice was kept intact, with every submitted contest entry on message.

Step Three

Give it away. One of the best ways to get the buzz buzzing about your product is to seed like you are crabgrass. Smart seeding is one of the most important aspects of word-of-mouth marketing. Once you have found the group that is most likely to jump on your bandwagon, wisely entice them with the promise of your product or service. Send free samples if you can; if that is not possible because of your price point, offer as big a discount as you can afford. Make the price as low as feasible to encourage people to give your product a try.

In 2004, the Chrysler brand was struggling. The manufacturers created the 300C, a hot new car with good buzz value. Daimler Chrysler loaned out the vehicles to a select number of people to help generate word of mouth. They chose consumers based on a profile, including those who were anticipating buying a new car within a year; who talk about the buying process; who were open to buying a domestic sedan; and those who had a wide social circle. Interestingly enough, being a Chrysler fan was not one of the requirements. In fact, the company's primary choices were not previous fans of the brand — the manufacturer did not want an existing loyalty to the product to undermine credibility. Those selected to drive the car must have spread good news about the vehicle because in one month, the seeding program landed 42 people behind the wheel of their newly purchased

300C. Beyond that, the follow-up survey to those who drove the vehicles showed that the average participant drove it more than 400 miles, toted an average of 14 total passengers, and had more than 60 conversations about the car. Now *there* is an example of how to drive a word-of-mouth campaign!

Or picture this: Nokia was preparing to unveil is 6682 SmartPhone but did not have the budget for a mass launch. The company wanted to get influential bloggers involved to help build awareness before the product was introduced to the marketplace. In a flash of inspiration, Nokia screened and recruited influential bloggers based on their lifestyle characteristics and not necessarily their technology prowess. The bloggers were seeded with a 6682 to help spread the word.

The numbers speak for themselves. Each influencer spoke, in person, to an average of 84 people but the online interactions present a more impressive picture. Within four weeks, a minimum of 193,000 blog visitors were exposed to posts about the product. Of the influencers, 73 percent became more interested in Nokia and its products, and 69 percent of them knew someone who bought or intended to buy the 6682 as a result of their influence. It was a picture-perfect word-of-mouth campaign.

Smaller businesses should not despair — you do not have to give away a massive amount of merchandise. At a basic level, simply pull together a "refer a friend" program and give your customers an incentive to do it. Consider this: A restaurant can cater to (pardon the pun) its regular customers, getting feedback from them and creating a discount program for each new diner they recruit. A hair salon may ask each of its clients to take a couple of cards to hand out to new potential prospects. The client can write his or her name on the card before giving it to someone else.

When that someone visits the salon, the owner knows exactly who brought that customer in and can offer a discounted haircut or other service.

It is easy to get caught up in targeting the same customers you typically focus on, but when it comes to successful seeding, get some new blood in the mix. Sure, you still need to target the usual suspects, but you should also consider reaching out to segments of the population in which you have few or no customers. Identify groups that are not likely to be familiar with your brand and seed them. You will be surprised at the growth you can experience.

You can also seed media outlets as long as it is done above-board. Try sending your product to the local weather person or news reporter. Radio disc jockeys have a tremendous reach and plenty of listeners. If they like what you send them, they may consider giving it a plug on the air. When it comes to a credible source like a local news personality saying positive things, it adds up to advertising you cannot buy.

As mentioned above, smart seeding can make all the difference in a word-of-mouth campaign. How can you ensure you are seeding the right influencers? Ironic as it may seem, it is somewhat like getting married.

Create your dream date. Just as Daimler Chrysler did, and define your target. Decide who is most likely to invest in your product and who has a broad circle of friends and family with whom to spread the word. Develop key criteria that will help you pinpoint the ideal customer. Once you have crafted your perfect brand ambassador (kind of like envisioning your dream date, except more realistic), find him or her. You can use new-fangled techniques like customer database mining or old-fashioned telephone interviews to identify your targets.

Act natural. It is important to gather your influencers together, but it needs to happen naturally. Try not to create formal, stiff environments where your influencers will meet and feel uncomfortable. Instead, look for opportunities to introduce them in a relaxed, natural setting where they may already gather together. If you are launching a new brand of hot dog, host a gathering at a ball park. Or, for those looking to stir up excitement about a new cooking utensil, get your group together at a food expo. The right setting makes all the difference in creating the appropriate tone and making people comfortable enough to talk.

Plan the guest list. You want to get enough people in one place to generate enthusiasm and excitement about your product, but it is a fine line. An intimate gathering often lacks the spark and energy of a bigger crowd. On the other hand, groups of too many people can feel unconnected. Remember how that wedding with 15 bridesmaids and 500 of the happy couple's closest friends seemed overdone? So does the launch with 300 of your closest influencers. Make them feel special to be part of the process.

Throw rice. Okay, not really, but that is one wedding tradition that involves the guests and makes them feel they are a part of the proceedings rather than just bystanders. If you just stand by and introduce your product, it probably will not be enough to get people to talk. Your gathering should engage your attendees. Have them play games. Get them holding the seed if possible so they get an instant impression within a favorable environment (Rice, seed. Get it?).

Give a well-written toast. When you are ready to reveal the product, the worst thing you can do is list every asset. Choose the three to five best features or selling points and develop your core message around them. No one likes a run-on toast from a drunken best man any more than they will like a pitch that seems never-ending. Keep it short, sweet, and on target.

Step Four

Pass it on. You need to give your talkers a way to spread the word. Whether it is a blog, a viral campaign, or a place for them to write reviews, provide a portal for people to communicate with each other. Bazaarblog and Keller Fay Research released a study that says fully 90 percent of people write reviews to help others make better buying decisions. If you give them a great product and a megaphone, people happily will shout about it.

Organic word of mouth typically spreads from person to person through conversation or online via email, blogs, and discussion boards or forums. Think of the various ways you communicate with friends and loved ones: that is organic word of mouth at work.

If you are aiming for the amplified variety, you help it along by creating communities, either online or off. The Internet itself is the prime way to achieve amplification — it is hard to imagine a way to get your message heard faster or louder than getting it online. You can use traditional or nontraditional publicity methods to create buzz and get people talking about you. You can write emails, blogs, or create viral messaging (more about those in upcoming chapters) to help WOM travel the world over.

Or you may choose to reach out to your influencers and get them using their own personal mouthpiece to spread the word to the masses. The spoken word is, after all, the essence of word of mouth. However you do it, both organic and amplified word of mouth require a product worth talking about and a way to share the information. Execute those two things well and great buzz will be waiting for you.

Step Five

Stay on track. It is not enough to get people to share information about your business. You need to know what they are saying and to whom. Track the buzz. After all, true conversation is based on talking and listening, so listen to what customers are saying about you. Use that to perfect your approach, and help spread your message even farther. Then strap on your seat belt and get ready to ride the wave of success.

That is what the Roaring Springs Water Park in Boise did. The park's marketing manager wanted to boost revenue but not necessarily the number of visitors. Afraid overcrowding would result in negative experiences, she wanted to get the season pass holders to come more often, stay longer at each visit, and spend more money.

After conducting face-to-face surveys with guests, feedback showed that people were dissatisfied with long lines, crowds, and a lack of available shade. The park quickly spent money to install more shade-producing structures, rework popular attractions to limit waiting times, and give season ticket holders extra special benefits.

As a result, Roaring Springs sold just 20 more tickets the following year but the changes reaped an additional $120,000 in revenue that year. Wisely, the park wanted to know what people thought and what they were saying, and by listening, created happier customers and better word of mouth.

Word of mouth is not a slam dunk. Unfortunately, many great products never get discovered by the masses and are left to collect dust on a shelf somewhere. The key is to keep creating buzz. If a word-of-mouth campaign fizzles at first, find a new way to get people talking. If you keep on it, someone may eventually pick up the ball and help you spread the word. Each time you generate interest, you increase your chances of a successful campaign.

BENEFITS OF WORD OF MOUTH

Author Andy Sernovitz sums it up pretty well when he lays out the benefits of this form of marketing. He says, "Word-of-mouth marketing is the most profitable marketing you can do. Nothing, I mean nothing, makes you more money." How can you turn away from that kind of promise? Just take a look at why word-of-mouth marketing works.

Your advertising does not have to cost a dime. Word of mouth is free. Watch how it works: Aunt Sal tells Uncle Saul, who tells his coworker, who tells the members of her bridge club, who tell their families, and the next thing you know, you have got the whole city clamoring for your product. Not bad for not investing a cent in buying ads.

No matter how small your start-up is, with a high-quality product you can generate enough word of mouth to put you over the top. Starbucks is a prime example. The Seattle-based coffee giant never advertised. It simply paired a great-tasting cup of coffee with a hip environment and let its customers do the rest.

There is no cost to acquire new customers. People are more connected than ever. They consistently talk via mobile media and the Internet. The average tech-savvy teen stores 94 phone numbers in a mobile phone and has 78 people on an instant-messenger buddy list, according to a study by MTV and Nickelodeon. That is a lot of opportunities to share a marketing morsel about your product or service, and you did not pay a dime for any of them.

More bang for your buck. If you do decide to launch a marketing campaign with ads, word of mouth reinforces the message you are sharing. People can refer back to your ads to give them extra legs. The same MTV Nickelodeon study mentioned above found that 47 percent of youth instant message each other about "what is on TV right now." A strong ad fans the flames of word-of-mouth marketing faster, and with positive results.

It levels the playing field. Remember the myth that those with the biggest budgets will succeed in marketing. Word of mouth is a perfect weapon for small business owners. In fact, when it comes to word-of-mouth marketing, small businesses can be giant players. It is easy to see why: Mom-and-pop companies are much more likely to know their customers than Macy's or Max Factor. The pharmacist at the store on the corner knows his customers by name. He also probably knows their families and maybe even their pets. Does the cashier at Nordstrom know — or care to know — yours?

In addition, smaller companies are closer to their clients. Beyond knowing their names and family histories, it is easier to track what people are saying when you know the people involved. If a long-time customer of that little mom-and-pop pharmacy is unhappy with a transaction, she will march her elephant-kneed stocking-clad self up to the owner and tell him exactly why. That same customer may attempt to explain her frustration to the cashier at CVS, but she is a lot less likely to be heard at the top of the corporate chain. What is the result? The small business owner has a chance to rectify the situation and squelch negative word of mouth; CVS may have just lost granny's business plus anyone she chooses to tell about her experience.

WHAT'S THE BUZZ?

Some people use the terms word-of-mouth marketing and buzz marketing synonymously. Throw other names like influencer marketing and viral marketing in, and you can concoct a word-of-mouth stew to rival the best Jambalaya. However, each has its own meaning.

It all begins with word-of-mouth marketing. Viral marketing is one approach to word-of-mouth. You will read more about it in Chapter 6, but for now, all you need to know is that viral marketing is creating an Internet message so compelling that people just have to pass it on (like a virus — get it?).

There is also influencer marketing, which, appropriately, involves finding influencers to help spread the word. Unlike buzz marketing, where marketers host an event to capture attention, influencer marketing involves revealing the product or service itself. An "influencer," who can be a blogger, VIP, celebrity, or some other person who has a large following, is allowed to test a product in the hopes that he or she will relay positive feedback about it to an audience.

Buzz marketing is another technique used to generate word of mouth. Marketers grab consumer's attention through an event or some sort of memorable action, hoping it will inspire them to talk it up. While buzz marketing may be an offshoot of word-of-mouth marketing, the key difference between the two terms is "marketing." Bottom line: Word-of-mouth marketing can generate buzz. Buzz marketing generates word of mouth.

Unlike traditional marketing, buzz, and word of mouth, influencer and viral marketing lay the advertising message in the hands of regular people rather than letting professionals work their magic. They are the brave new world in which the public decides what messages are worth sharing and when and how to share them. You will read more about each of these other forms in other chapters. For our purposes, the two terms, buzz and word of mouth, will be used interchangeably.

No matter whether you draw a line between the buzz and word-of-mouth marketing, or whether you choose to lump them together, there is a distinct difference between them and what is known as shill, guerilla, undercover, or stealth marketing. These latter terms are defined as a definite attempt to hide that someone is affiliated with a company that he or she is representing, which beautifully leads to the next point.

A WORD ABOUT ETHICS

Despite your political views, ethics is not a four-letter word. Keeping your word-of-mouth marketing honest is crucial to successfully selling your product or service. Ethics will be covered more in Chapter 10, but in the meantime, remember this key rule:

Talk candidly. Do not try to hide drawbacks, side effects, or potential pitfalls when getting the word out. People will decide for themselves whether they like your product or service. If for some reason they do not love it but you have been honest from the start, they probably will not hold it against your company. However, if you have not been upfront, you just irreparably damaged your credibility — and your chances for total success. As Emanuel Rosen wrote in his foreword for *Connected Marketing*, "Full disclosure is a prerequisite to good buzz marketing. Not only because undercover campaigns can backfire, but first and foremost because full disclosure is the right thing to do."

After-Word

1. Word-of-mouth marketing is basically the practice of customer referrals on steroids. Nothing is more powerful that the recommendation of a trusted source.

2. People are so inundated with advertising messages, they do not pay attention to them. When they do listen, they do not believe. That is the reason word-of-mouth marketing is so much more effective.

3. Two kinds of word-of-mouth marketing exist: organic and amplified. Organic happens naturally, with people just generically telling others about a good product or experience. Amplified occurs when a company helps to encourage that conversation by giving out incentives or rewards.

4. Traditional marketing fails in today's marketplace because it is outdated and too expensive. It is also based on business practices that do not exist anymore.

5. There are five basic components to a word-of-mouth marketing campaign. They include finding the right people, developing a strong message, getting your product

in the hands of people who will talk, giving them a way to spread the word, and tracking what they say.

6. Word of mouth is beneficial because it is highly effective. It is free or low-cost marketing. It does not cost you anything to acquire new customers. Finally, if you do decide to use traditional advertising, it only enhances the buzz you are creating.

7. There are different terms for word-of-mouth marketing; some are interchangeable and some are not. Terms you never want to use to describe (or hear about) your marketing campaign include shill, guerilla, or stealth. These are undercover, underhanded techniques that are unethical and sometimes illegal. Be honest and transparent and reap the benefits of good word of mouth!

THE C-WORD

NOTHING is more important to building a word-of-mouth marketing campaign than the customer. You can develop the best marketing strategy out there but without a satisfied customer to spread the word, that product will linger on the lot like a Charlie Brown Christmas tree.

Take care of your customer, though, and they will do the marketing for you. They will buy your product or service, they will tell others about your product or service, and they may even become your biggest cheerleaders (pom-pons are optional).

This chapter examines:

- Why customer service has to come first

- The customer-generated sales force

- Building your sales force

- Customer evangelists

- Loyalty programs

CARE AND FEEDING OF YOUR CUSTOMER

No matter how terrific your product is, or no matter how revolutionary or how earth-shattering, if people do not buy it, you are out of luck and business. At the risk of sounding overly dramatic, customers — the "C-Word" — are the life-blood of any venture: more important than the company's CEO, its reputation, or the product it sells. Certainly, all of the above are also critical elements, but without a buyer, you simply cannot stay in business.

Yet this basic principle is all too often overlooked. As you develop a plan, a product, and all of the essentials that go along with growing your company, it is far too easy to ignore this integral part of your business. After all, you have to focus on how to make your product the best it can be, how to market it, how to pay your staff (or yourself), and how to turn your business into the next Big Thing. Customers just happen, right? They will see your gizmo and will be all a-twitter to buy it. They will not be able to help themselves any more than Dolly Parton at a beauty salon. So, do not pay them any attention — unless you want to actually see your business succeed. If you do, cater to them. Cultivate them and care about them, because they can make or break you faster than a plate in a Spode-throwing event in a parking lot.

Taking care of your customers, then, has to be your ultimate priority even before you engage in word-of-mouth marketing. No matter whether you are a start-up upstart or an established player in the marketplace, you need to put your customers first.

CASE STUDY: BRIAN COESTER

Brian Coester, President

Coester Appraisal Group

www.coesterappraisals.com

888-485-1999 - phone

301-231-8275 - fax

We used to spend time and money marketing for new clients, asking for referrals, and prospecting — with little success. We spent $25,000 a year on advertising, sometimes through direct mail, sometimes on the Web and with Google, but we never saw a return on investment. Then we got the idea that if we focused less on landing new clients and more on improving the service to our existing ones the word would get out and we would grow.

The first thing we did was to make sure that someone was always at the office to answer the phone within two rings. It is common in our industry to have no one answer the phone and just let all calls go to voice mail. We also made sure the office staff had the power to make things happen. We equipped them to handle every conceivable question so customers were not waiting for someone to call them back.

We hired more people in key locations and expanded our coverage area to include all of Washington, D.C., Virginia, and Maryland. That way we never had to turn down potential business or give people a reason to go looking for another company. It made us a one-stop shop for our customers. This alone helped tremendously because our clients now have one source, which they really like.

Finally, we stepped up our communication. We automated our entire process so that customers always know the status of their appraisal. They get daily updates via email notices, which also inform them if there is anything they need to act on. It cut our phone calls and email in half, saving us valuable time to be more productive for our customers.

CASE STUDY: BRIAN COESTER

Our phone never stops ringing now. We spend maybe $1,000 a year on advertising, mainly for pens, note pads, and brochures and business cards. We get a tremendous amount of business through referrals because of our service. We are big on follow-ups and always make sure to go the extra mile for our clients. It's really kind of simple; we just do business better than our competitors.

Think about the last time you felt that a business listened to you or did something that benefited you even if it required a sacrifice on their part. I recently fell in love with a small paint-your-own pottery store in my home town (which was a surprise because I have always been better with antonyms then acrylics). I started a project there on a Saturday and I was gung-ho determined to get it done that week despite a crazy schedule. I called them one evening and asked the saleswoman how late the store was open. She responded, "We're not open but I am here so if you want to finish your piece, just come on by." I was shocked! Most people would have told me what time the store reopened the next day, but this woman was willing to let me come in while they were closed so that I could do something I was really excited about. After all, she was already there so what did it matter whether she had a little company? And yet most businesses would have gone the traditional route and not allowed me in after hours. This one did, and I got the rush of finishing a really cool project, and at the same time, felt like someone did something really special for me. I told several people about my experience and I am certain some of them gave this little place a try as a result. That experience combined customer care with word-of-mouth marketing all at once.

Being responsive is also key. While researching this book, I read several things about Maxine Clark, the founder of the Build-a-Bear Workshops. Everything I read explained how much emphasis she puts on customer service. I wanted to interview her for a case study and so I decided to contact her. She is purported to answer her own emails, which I found hard to believe, but I sent an email with my request to her, confident that weeks would pass before I would receive a canned response from some assistant. Not only did she herself answer her email but she did it within three hours, graciously accepting my request for an interview. Three hours! She is the head of a million-dollar enterprise and it took her less time to answer than it does for my sinus medicine to work. I was amazed — and became an instant customer even though I have never stuffed my own bear. If she ever decided to run for president, I may even volunteer to head up her campaign. That is how much I thought of her quick response. The point of my little love fest for Maxine: She created a believer by being responsive, and in doing so, I am now spreading word of mouth on her behalf.

Contrast that to an experience I had on a one-day bus jaunt to Atlantic City. (No, I am not bitter just because I coughed up more money than a cat does hairballs.) My two sisters, my mother, and I had the bus ride from hell. First, the driver was about a half-hour late. Then, he realized about an hour into the trip that he had forgotten his wallet (driving an entire bus full of people without your driver's license is not recommended). He made arrangements for someone to retrieve it and meet him in a parking lot to give it to him, which meant we had to wait for him — again. Roughly another 45 minutes passed while we sat, stopped in a desolate lot until his comrade brought it to him. Finally, we were on the road again.

You would think that after waiting all of that time, we would be thrilled just to be moving. You would be wrong. We were praying the whole time simply to survive the ride. The driver drove more recklessly than a New York City cab driver, speeding, swerving, and swearing the entire trip. He never even slowed down for speed bumps. You may never have experienced being on a bus going full tilt over a speed bump, and I hope you never do, but let me tell you: it requires a good deal of Advil afterwards. Our heads hit the ceiling at about 45 miles an hour. We made it to the casino in one piece (which is saying quite a bit) but also about an hour and a half behind schedule.

The story goes on, including his refusal to let a handicapped woman board early for the return trip and several other infractions that could likely fill an entire book on how not to get ahead in the travel industry. Suffice it to say, it was an all-around horrible experience and one I hope never to repeat. The four of us each decided to write letters of complaint about the driver to ensure the company knew of the problems we encountered.

Only one of us received a response. And, surprise, surprise, it was my sister who had written her missive and printed it out while she was on the job at the law firm where she worked. Therefore, a letter printed on legal letterhead prompted a reaction but the three of us who worked in less visible places got nada, zip, and zilch in response. Imagine that.

We still make several trips to Atlantic City every year but we have never used that particular service again. If the bus company had at least had the decency to respond, to apologize, or to offer restitution in some form, we would have given them a second chance. The old saying, "You never get a second chance to make a first impression" rings loudly as I write this. Of course, so does "Put your money where your mouth is," but if you have ever seen how dirty your hands get after a day of playing slot machines, you probably would think twice about it.

The moral of the story: You may not like what people have to say about you, but you had better, at the very least, respond. They at least had the courage to tell you about a problem. Results from the Retail Customer Dissatisfaction Study 2006 showed that only 6 percent of shoppers who experienced a problem with a retailer contacted the company. Only 6 percent! A whopping 31 percent of people went on to tell family, friends, and colleagues about a dissatisfying experience. Of those, 8 percent told one person, another 8 percent told two people, and 6 percent told six or more people about a problem. There is that 6 percent again, but this time, 6 percent equals a lot more lost business. The study showed that if 100 people all have a bad experience at a retailer, that store stands to lose between 32 and 36 current or potential customers. Remember, word-of-mouth marketing works both ways.

So consider yourself lucky if a dissatisfied client speaks up; at least you have the chance to make things right. Let them know you heard them. If your company was at fault, own up to it and offer to try to make it right. Even if you disagree and feel the company did nothing wrong, acknowledge the customer's feedback. Thank them for sharing it. Tell them you appreciate their patronage and you hope they will do business with you again. Most people just want to be heard. Listen to them and then let your ears perk up at the sweet sound of good buzz.

That does not mean it will be a pleasant experience. No one I know likes to hear someone say something negative about them or their business. Sometimes, though, the message can have a profound effect. I have a friend, Ed Watson, who owned a Dunkin' Donuts franchise for a long time in southern Maryland. For the first three years, he was robbing Peter to pay Paul simply to stay afloat. He sometimes handed out paychecks on Friday but asked the employees not to cash them until Monday just so he could use the weekend sales to cover the payroll.

One day, he was talking to one of his regular customers, griping about trying to do the bills while making donuts, working the cash register, and waiting on those coming in to buy a dozen treats. He was multitasking to the max and not enjoying it at all. His customer said something that rocked his world. He told Ed, "Your attitude sucks," or something to that effect. Ed was stunned, especially because he always catered to this particular patron. The remark stayed with him all day and he really took it to heart. Ed realized he needed to change his focus from simply keeping his business running to actually catering to his customers.

He decided to make his little Dunkin' Donuts an oasis, a destination if you will, where people would want to come to catch their breath and escape from the stresses of everyday life. They could never feel that if they walked in and sensed Ed's own stress. It was a huge turning point for his business, as sales took off. Ed never looked back, except to thank his customer for opening his eyes to what he should have seen in the first place — he was in business because of his customers, not in spite of them.

There is no question that it is hard for new businesses to juggle it all. They may not have many customers to begin with, which is why it is imperative that they keep every single one of them happy. They cannot afford to lose even one. I am not advocating that every business stay open past hours to accommodate a customer (although how cool would it be if they did?) or that any other extreme measures be taken. Companies that follow the good old-fashioned advice to be responsive will enjoy good word of mouth as a result. Return phone calls or emails, even if you do not have an answer to a query. Respond and let someone know you are checking on it. If you have a miscommunication or a misstep, follow up and try to make it right. Let people know you are serious about giving them a satisfactory experience.

When it comes right down to it, businesses are built on reputation, not on sales. Build a good reputation and people will support you to the best of their ability. Get a bad rep and it is hard to sell a damn thing.

The point is that every customer is valuable and every one of them offers the potential to share word of mouth about a business, good or bad. Why not ensure it is good?

Beyond customer satisfaction is customer retention. Customers can support your business in so many ways beyond buying your goods and services. Some say that customers fall into the 80/20 rule: 80 percent of your business comes from 20 percent of your customers. Regardless of the fraction, the point remains that when you cultivate a customer, you are cultivating your business every bit as much.

- As little as a 5 percent increase in customer retention can boost your profits by 25 to 100 percent. You could double your bottom line profit by keeping only 5 percent of the customers you currently lose.

- Seventy-three percent of customers base their repurchasing decisions on the quality of service they received when problems occurred.

- Customers are willing to pay up to 10 percent more for excellent service.

- A 1 percent increase in loyalty equals a 10 percent cost reduction.

- The probability of selling to existing customers is 60 to

70 percent. Contrast that to 5 to 20 percent likelihood of selling to a new prospect.

- Customer loyalty accounts for 38 percent of margin, 40 percent of revenue growth and 38 percent of shareholder value.

The numbers tell the story far better than I ever could. Customers will continue to buy from a business that treats them right, and the business will benefit ten-fold.

That said, how can you turn a buyer into a motivator?

CASE STUDY: MAXINE CLARK

Build-a-Bear Workshop

1954 Innerbelt Business Center Drive.

St. Louis, MO 63114-5760

www.buildabear.com

314-423-8000 - phone

314-423-8188 - fax

Maxine Clark, Chief Executive Bear

Word of mouth has played a huge role in our success. In the beginning (1997) we started with one store in St. Louis and we had no budget for marketing. One by one customers came in and had a great time, and they would share that with others.

If you give people a so-so product they won't talk about it. But if you want to create an evangelist for your product, it is all about their connection. We connect with our guests. We create an environment to give people the best possible experience they could have. It is not service, necessarily; it is being engaged with the customers.

CASE STUDY: MAXINE CLARK

We didn't start advertising nationally until late fall of 2003. We were depending on buzz and customer recommendations until then. We now have over 300 locations nationwide.

When we opened, we had a few customers every day for a little while. The magic moment for me was the day after Thanksgiving, when we got there at 6:00 a.m. and there was a line out the door already. I thought people would just buy gift cards but people came into the stores with their children to make their bears, and they made it a tradition over the years.

We sell the brand experience. It is more than a product; it is the fun and unforgettable memories of making your own stuffed animal, which are every bit as important as the product. When we started Build-a-Bear, I wanted it to be all about the good things remember as a child, when I went shopping with my mom. It was not about the stuff, I just remember how nice people were to me when we came to the department store dining room. They made me feel special. My business focus is to create special memories for my customers and in turn, they'll spend more money.

Word of mouth has to be genuine. It can't be contrived. Customers will sense it right away and I think that's a good thing. It makes all of us be on our toes. Nothing is hidden anymore. People will read things from their friends and they'll share what is on their minds.

THE CUSTOMER-GENERATED SALES FORCE

Loyal customers can become an essential part of your marketing efforts if they feel that they are valued. View every person as a customer for life and treat them that way. They are likely to live up to it if you do and equally likely to encourage family and friends to join their ranks.

That includes giving them something they did not expect. A dear friend of mine is a personal chef. She also caters dinner parties and prepares precooked meals. (Did I mention I am not much of a cook? Is it any wonder she is a dear friend?) Each time she does an event, she includes a small surprise as her way of thanking a client for the business. For instance, when she catered a small dinner party, she snuck a tray of brandy and cigars into the library when the guests were gathered in the dining room. When she prepared a Christmas Eve feast for one family, she included a jar of homemade cocoa powder with candy cane bits for the hosts to enjoy on Christmas morning. And when she created an intimate dinner for two, she left fresh-squeezed orange juice and champagne in the fridge so the couple would also have a special way to start the next day.

As a business owner, think about how you can surprise your customers with an unexpected treat. A florist may deliver a single rose as a thank-you gift to the person who ordered a flower arrangement. A wedding photographer could include a free sheet of wallet-sized pictures for the happy couple's parents. Make it your mission to simply write a thank-you note to one customer each day. Your gesture does not have to cost much but it will make clients remember the exceptional service, which is key to generating a customer sales force.

Jack Baum, owner of Canyon Cafes, a Dallas-based restaurant chain, offers pats on the back to acquire more loyal customers. He scours the local newspapers daily, looking for announcements that employees have been promoted. He then sends the employee a congratulatory letter and encourages them to come for a visit to enjoy free champagne or wine to celebrate the accomplishment. The program became such a hit with Southwest Airlines employees that Baum was able to finagle a trade: free dinners in exchange for free airline tickets, which he gave away as contest prizes. He started the practice in the '90s and people are still talking about it.

While I have never gotten an invitation from Mr. Baum (it is hard for freelance authors to get promotions), a local real estate agent made a smart move that certainly caught my attention. He apparently looks through the birth announcements in the local paper to see who has just had a new baby. Naturally, many people who have just expanded their family need to expand their house, so it is a key market for realtors. Knowing that a birth announcement is a highly prized and personal keepsake, this agent cut out my son's announcement, laminated it, and sent it to me with his business card and a congratulatory note. It was both smart marketing and a great way to let people know he exists. Of course I told family and friends about the gesture and for what cost him pennies, he generated some great word of mouth.

Think about how you can surprise and delight customers and potential customers. Conjure up something totally unexpected and beyond the norm. Then clean out your ears so you will be able to hear the sweet sounds of people talking about your business.

BUILDING YOUR SALES FORCE

Developing your customer-led sales force is based on common sense. First, get customers to participate when you are rolling out new products. Actively seek and listen to their input. Ask them to join advisory panels or test new merchandise. Anything that makes them feel like part of the team. When iRobot Corporation introduced Roomba, the robot vacuum that learns to avoid furniture and starts cleaning at preset times, the company thought it was creating a tool to help people. Then customers proved that they saw Roomba as an extension of the family, often giving their robot elaborate paint jobs and even naming their vacuum. The company saw potential to foster a customer sales force. iRobot encouraged Roomba owners to invent new uses for the vacuum. It even gave them a place to show off their "pet" at **www.irobot.com/create/ explore**, a Web site that features customers' latest inventions.

JetBlue Airways created a customer sales force out of college students. For several years, the airline has sent dozens of students back to school in September with an assortment of freebies and incentives to encourage classmates to book a flight. Beyond the incentives, the students promote JetBlue on blogs and Facebook to help spread the word.

Serious horse lovers know all about the Parelli organization, a company that teaches natural horsemanship, where the human learns the skills to ride and not the other way around. To spread its message even farther, the group tours across the United States and gives members of its official Parelli International Savvy Club up to ten free tickets to events. The club members hand out the passes to attract new prospects to join the Parelli movement. By putting the passes in club members' hands instead of the company sending them out blindly, Parelli followers feel as though they are sharing something special. They have a gift to give to someone they know or care about, making them feel important and part of a team all at the same time. Giving them the power to share their passion adds an extra level of loyalty.

With a growing emphasis on going green, Vespa Scooters are getting more popular. Piaggio Group Americas, Inc. conducted a two-month contest in 2007 to encourage owners and fans of the scooters to show their brand devotion and to demonstrate the scooter's contributions to a healthier environment. To help spread the word about how Vespas helps curb global warming, decrease traffic congestion, and make a style statement, drivers and devotees were asked to create original videos demonstrating Vespa's attributes. The three best videos were selected and their creators were awarded a new scooter, with multiple runners-up receiving Vespa apparel.

With one two-month contest, Vespa managed to further brand awareness and increase visibility all while getting its "Vespanomics" message heard: The scooter is better for the environment and the pocketbook. Beyond that, the company engaged its customers to help spread word of mouth instead of a paid sales force.

Once you have assembled your sales force, bring them together. Find reasons for your customers to meet. Whether you are selling real estate or Ginsu knives, getting your most loyal fan base together at a conference or meeting helps foster the feeling of being part of something bigger than them. Better yet, throw a party for the customers themselves to show how much you value them. It does not have to cost a fortune but you will gain a mint in good buzz. They share their energy, and take that spark back out into the trenches with them, dripping nuggets of free publicity for you everywhere they go.

At Macworld 2007, the Mac Business Unit at Microsoft sponsored a "Blogger Lounge," where aficionados could meet. The lounge offered free, fast Internet access and a comfortable place for people to write about their experiences at Macworld. The goal? To support the Mac blogger communities, increase MacBU's visibility within those communities, and give bloggers a chance to meet their Microsoft counterparts. Simply by providing a few leather couches, six computers, and some refreshments, Microsoft averaged 50 lounge visitors per day, four video podcasts, and nearly 100 posts mentioning the lounge — posts on sites that were linked to by another 7,000 blogs. Not bad exposure for a gathering of Microsoft rebels at a Mac event!

Re-educate your staff. Remind them that the customer comes first. Reinforce that the customer is always right. You cannot afford for one employee to be rude to a customer. You will not only lose that person's business, but it is also likely you will lose even more because they will share their bad experience with others. On the other hand, if you cater to your customers and make them feel that they are important to you, you create an unparalleled brand loyalty. Lucky Strike knows the benefits of that. The all-but-dead brand of cigarettes launched a "Lucky Strike Force," targeting smokers who feel ostracized and literally left out in the cold. Staff members in trendy neighborhoods like Miami's South Beach and New York's Soho offered hot coffee to shivering smokers who huddled outside during the winter. In the summertime, they proffered lounge chairs and iced coffee to make the smokers banished to the outdoors more comfortable. To smokers who felt that they were viewed as second-class citizens because of their habit, the campaign made them feel wanted, valued, and appreciated, and ultimately helped boost a brand in dire need of some good word of mouth.

Keep in touch. A single phone call, letter, or even an email keeps you on the radar, and may be just the reminder needed to place an order with you. I take my very hairy canine to a local groomer a few times a year. The company recently called to remind me that it had been more than 12 weeks since her last appointment. With a hectic schedule and too many deadlines, I had totally overlooked the fact that she was due for an extreme makeover. The phone call was not a solicitation, it was a simple reminder. The groomer was not pushy in any way, and yet that single phone call solidified my relationship with that particular business. I felt that they cared.

Next time you are wondering how to touch base with a client, drop a birthday card in the mail, or send an anniversary card marking their first transaction with you. It will do wonders for your relationship.

Remember, return customers equal return dollars. Invest wisely.

MICROSHARING

Sometimes loyal customers can be cultivated through something called microsharing, which is basically the same as a clique in middle school but without the bad feelings and bubble gum. Unlike your eighth-grade class, however, the goal of microsharing is to spread a message far and wide — it simply uses a select group of people to do it.

Rohit Bhargava, blogger and senior vice president of Digital Strategy and Marketing at Ogilvy Public Relations, called microsharing a phenomenon "that brands need to start paying more attention to, because of the impact it has on public perception about their brand."

As individuals share pieces of information or content with others who have similar needs or interests (for example, the pesky middle school clique), they can determine what and how much information to share. They are akin to the business middleman; the company produces a product, the middleman decides how and when to market it, and the consumer snaps it up. Microsharing is an important aspect of word-of-mouth marketing, in that if you successfully target a group of loyal customers to share your campaign, you give them the satisfaction of being closely linked to your brand. You also give them the power to distribute information about your product or service with the masses.

Engaging your loyal customers through microsharing is not only smart, it is crucial to building your word-of-mouth campaign.

COMMUNITY MARKETING

Another smart way to build a loyal customer force is to focus on your current customers' needs through what is sometimes called community marketing. It has been defined as online niche communities and publications that create lasting relationships between community members and brands. Essentially that means it connects existing customers to other current clients, as well as to prospects. It also solidifies a business's connection to its core supporters, and lets prospective customers communicate with each other. In short, it gets everyone talking about you and your product or service.

Many companies are leveraging community marketing via blogs or corporate Web sites, and you will read more about those in upcoming chapters. Yahoo! Groups is one example where people who share an interest can interact online. YouTube, Facebook, Twitter, and other social networking sites are other great places for community marketing (and are thoroughly covered in Chapter 9). Fan clubs and discussion forums are rife with community marketing examples.

What if I said you could generate your own community market via a membership site? Not a company's Web site, mind you, but a site that targets your customers, where they can actively discuss your industry. Once a few members of your target audience are aware it exists, they will pass along the information to others who share their interests. Zap! You have created an online community market.

Now, you simply get a couple of people within that community to try your product or service. If they like it, if it helps them in any way, they are sure to hotfoot it over to their computer to share the news. And the people they are sharing it with are the prospects most likely to need your business. Pow! More potential customers know about you, talk about you, and give your company a try. Zowie! Word of mouth and increased sales. (And you thought only Batman could use those terms effectively.)

THE CUSTOMER EVANGELIST

An evangelist is not the same as a loyal customer. A loyal customer patronizes a business time and time again. An evangelist is a consumer who is so passionate about a company that he or she spends his or her free time or money trying to help grow that business. Evangelists believe in the company and its people. They offer unsolicited praise and share their positive viewpoint with anyone and everyone who will listen. In addition, they do not, in any way, want to receive compensation to do so. They simply love a company or a product and will do anything and everything they can to help it succeed.

Customer evangelists are the key to rallying the public to your bully pulpit. Much like the crazy Southern Baptist youth director you read about earlier, they spread your message far and wide (but without turning off their intended audience in a crowded parking lot). They are a group of satisfied believers, cheerleaders, or influentials that can be converted into a potent marketing force.

Evangelists frequently devise their own campaign without any marketing aids. Mike Kaltschnee is also known as the Hacking Netflix blogger. He began the Web site **www.HackingNetflix.**

com in 2003 to dole out helpful advice to other Netflix members to help them maximize their use of the by-mail DVD rental service. He offers tips and tricks to site visitors and his Web site is the second highest result on Google searches for Netflix — surpassed only by the official company Web site.

Hally Cokenias made it her mission to sprinkle a product called Bacon Salt across the globe. The seasoning, produced by J&D's Down Home Enterprises LLC in Washington State, makes food taste like bacon. Cokenias dressed up as the Bacon Salt Fairy for Halloween and sprinkled the product on other guests' food. She touched base with the company founders via email, and they wisely responded, solidifying an already strong bond. Due to her love of the product and a good impression of the company's leadership, Cokenias became even more of an evangelist, mailing several bottles to friends across the globe to give others a taste of her favorite new seasoning.

Lynette Chiang is the customer evangelist for Green Gear Cycling, based in Eugene, Oregon. The company custom-crafts folding travel bicycles and hosts the Bike Friday Club of America, where owners, friends, and aficionados who love their bicycles meet up for rides in their local area. Each time a Bike Friday leader hosts an event, Chiang takes it upon herself to email all bicycle riders within a 60-mile radius to spread the word about the ride and promote the company. Anyone can ride, no matter what kind of bicycle they own. The company also gives its riders referral cards to hand out to anyone who asks about the odd-looking cycle with the small wheels. Those who send referral cards in to the company receive money or product discounts for helping to spread the word. Talk about giving word of mouth some legs!

Phil Peterson is known as the Mac evangelist. He achieved the title by penning more than one million bulletin board posts online to support Apple, most of them directed to Windows users who were experiencing difficulties. Peterson would respond to queries for help by suggesting the poster change computers. His answers ranged from "You wouldn't have that problem if you used a Mac," to "I wouldn't know. I use a Mac," and his very famous post, "They ripped that off the Mac." He "retired" as a customer evangelist in 2007 and Mac is still working out the bugs of finding another cheerleader to take his place.

Not that Walt Disney needs customer evangelists to further its brand, but the company has an unrivaled one in George Reiger. He has been called the number one devoted Disney fan of all time. As of October, 2006, he sported more than 1,900 Disney tattoos all over his body. He reportedly gets three to four new tats every week. And if being a walking Walt were not enough, every inch of his 4,200 square foot, custom-built Disney home houses one of his 26,000 Disney collectibles. If you can beat that, I am all ears.

Syndicated radio talk-show host Glenn Beck is a Coke Zero evangelist. Beck not only apparently loves the product but he touts it fairly regularly on his show, "The Glenn Beck Program," which airs on more than 260 radio stations. Coca-Cola decided to respond to his glowing comments with a letter and a supply of the soft drink, which somehow never made it to Beck. He made an even bigger deal about the missing soda and letter, chatting about the product on the air for more than five minutes one day. Beck invited a Coke Zero spokesperson to his studio and the two discussed the product at length over the airwaves. The radio personality made it clear that he was voluntarily promoting the product with no payment simply because he really enjoyed it. Talk about a bubbling endorsement!

Finally, Mark Malkoff showed off his brand evangelism for Ikea by literally moving into the store. When Malkoff had to vacate his apartment for a week while it was being fumigated, the Paramus, New Jersey comedian took up residence in his local Ikea. Clearly he could have spent a luxurious week on a vacation or rented a ritzy room in a hotel, but he approached Ikea about being a live-in shopper and the company wisely agreed. It translated into all kinds of word of mouth, including extensive media coverage. Local school groups made field trips to see Malkoff hanging out in his showroom/living room or kicking back in his faux bedroom. It was an ingenious way for the retailer to show it carries everything you need to feel at home, while catering to one of its die-hard brand ambassadors. It is a good thing the store had a shower available in the executive office.

Loyalty Programs

Sometime evangelists develop on their own; other times a company can cultivate a passionate customer into an evangelist. Like Maker's Mark. The bourbon's makers toasted the bright idea to create the Maker's Mark Ambassadors, a club for their most cherished customers. On the company's Web site, visitors can download personalized Maker's Mark business cards to give out. As ambassadors they can have their name engraved on a barrel of bourbon, and attend local and national events hosted by Maker's Mark. Rather than worry about the masses, the company chooses to foster its relationship with its most loyal customers, leaving them to spread the word about how much they love their bourbon of choice.

Threadless (**www.threadless.com**) is an online T-shirt printer and seller with enthusiastic brand ambassadors. The company asks customers to submit ideas for images they wanted to see printed on T-shirts. The site's users get to vote on each of the images submitted and the company picks which ones to print based on the process. Double bonus points: Threadless managed to involve its fans in submitting the images and voting on them. The members who submit winning designs are awarded cash or other prizes. Triple bonus points: The site's users also tells the company whether they would be willing to purchase the product, so Threadless has a good idea of what kind of sales to expect before ever spending a dime on a new design.

You would not think people could get too jazzed up about scissors, but you would be wrong. Fiskars, a popular craft and scrapbooking scissors brand, wanted to build a community of 200 "Fiskateers." The company sought four part-time, paid ambassadors to become intimately acquainted with the brand and the product. After an intense weekend of education at the Fiskars headquarters in Wisconsin, the chosen four went back to their communities to blog, attend tradeshows, teach classes, and build awareness about the Fiskateers. Within five months, there were 815 members in 45 states creating their own marketing tools and planning events. Now there is a sharp idea.

Del Monte Foods created its own online community called "I Love My Dog," which contains roughly 400 members who were hand-licked, I mean, hand-picked to join the private network. The company turns to this online group of evangelists for help in creating products, test-marketing campaigns, and creating word of mouth. When the manufacturer decided to create a new breakfast treat for dogs, it went straight to the online group faster than a dog greets a mailman, asking members what they most wanted to feed their pets in the morning. The public responded that they wanted to give their pets bacon-and-egg-flavored treats, so Del Monte created Snausages Breakfast Bites. The ability to correspond quickly substantially shortened the product development cycle; where it typically takes more than a year from the time the company creates an idea to the product landing on store shelves, Snausages Breakfast Bites took only six months to make the cycle.

Del Monte went beyond getting initial product ideas from its network, however. During the time period it took to create the new treats, the company contacted members dozens of times to get feedback and input. It also utilized its members for pre-launch word of mouth. The move worked, helping to remove some of the unknowns for marketers, giving consumers more control over their choices, and taking some of the guesswork out of the equation of new product launches.

Evangelists can have a mighty impact on your business. Think about it — beyond the fact that they are offering free and unparalleled PR for your company, they are also more likely to be heard than a typical marketing machine. Remember: people trust other people. If you can get evangelists working on your side, you have got a powerful tool in your word-of-mouth arsenal.

DEVELOPING A LOYALTY PROGRAM

The above examples show just how effective brand ambassadors can be. If you are one of the lucky businesses with self-appointed evangelists who are touting your product all on their own, congratulations! If you need a little help to develop a few of these walking business gold mines, read on.

First things first: Figure out who deserves to be part of your program. Which customers frequent your business most? Who spends the most money? The two will not always be the same. Use a database to track visits and spending and develop your program with these loyal customers in mind.

Once you have targeted your best customers, decide how you are going to reward them. Will you implement a frequent buyer program? Maybe you would rather offer incentives for repeat customers or reward certain spending amounts. Whether you decide to reward by multiple visits or amount spent, make it an attainable and realistic goal. No one will be enticed by a seemingly impossible figure. You may even consider stair-stepping your program; the more people buy, the more incentive they receive. This is a great way to increase sales during the slower times of the year.

Next you will need to figure out what you will give them as a reward for their continued business. It can be anything from store credit, to cash back, to gifts, or free merchandise. Depending on your business, perhaps it makes sense to consider offering a discount or a special upgrade. The incentive needs to be a good one — do not skimp here or your customers will not be enticed. Nor will they feel particularly special, which is what you are aiming for. Think about added incentives for the first customers to join your program; it will give consumers a reason to jump in to your program quickly.

Now it is time to spread the good news about your loyalty program. Extend an invitation that really makes your customers feel they are part of something very special. You can issue this invitation through direct mail or email. In this case, a very formal letter or invite can exude a prestige that an email will not match, but it will depend on your budget. You should also include a mention of your loyalty program in any marketing effort you launch.

As with any form of word-of-mouth marketing, you need to set goals for your program and measure your results. If you are not seeing increasing interest and sales after you implement the program, you may need to revise or increase the incentives you are offering. Monitor how many people are signing up for your program. Track the number of sales that are tied to your loyal customers.

Finally, consider a referral bonus. Any loyal customer who brings in new business will get an added incentive. Knowing they will get a bigger discount or free merchandise is a powerful inducement to people to recruit friends and family. And after all, sharing the excitement is the basis of word-of-mouth marketing at its core.

YOUR OTHER LOYAL SALES FORCE

Do not overlook the other crucial part of your sales force: your staff. Your employees need to be evangelists too. If they are not, you are missing a valuable sales tool. Treat your employees like gold. Get them excited about your product, your mission, and your company. If they believe that what you are offering is the best thing since sliced bread, they are more likely to sell more loaves. If you do not rev up your employees' passion for sharing your product, your business is toast.

Beyond getting employees excited about your business, nurture their involvement in your company. Regardless of whether you have a staff of ten or 10,000, each one of your workers needs to be on the same page. Whether you accomplish that by a company email newsletter, monthly bulletin, or internal blog, it is imperative you share information with your staff and they have a mouthpiece to voice their concerns. Keeping your employees engaged and excited goes a long way toward promoting good word of mouth. After all, if you are focusing on generating good buzz among the public but your staff is bad-mouthing you at the same time, your chances of creating a successful campaign are about as good as Willie Nelson lining up for a haircut. It just will not happen.

The key is to consider your employees as every bit as valuable as your customers. In 2007, The Dow Chemical Company launched a blog penned by the company's chairman and CEO, Andrew Liveris. Named "Access Andrew," the goal was to communicate Liveris' vision and make him more accessible to employees. He wrote his own entries with minimal editing or input from the communications or legal teams. He posted new entries roughly every ten days and invited employees to respond with comments and concerns. The approach worked. In the first week it was live, more than 27,000 employees visited the blog and more than 11,000 staff members still check it weekly. Nearly 600 employees have posted more than 800 comments since the site launched. In a follow-up survey conducted after the first month of "Access Andrew," 77 percent of employees said they felt the blog had enhanced employee communications at Dow.

NETWORKING

In addition to customers, a strong sales staff can make all the difference in getting your company noticed. What if you are a small business that cannot spend a fortune on sales people? Try local networking groups. They are one of the best ways to find built-in salespeople for your business.

CASE STUDY: MARK AMTOWER

Federal Direct

Box 314, Highland, Maryland 20777

www.federaldirect.com

www.epiphanybook.com

amtower@erols.com

301-924-0058 - phone

Mark Amtower - Founding Partner

Author - *Government Marketing Best Practices*, **2004, and**

Why Epiphanies Never Occur to Couch Potatoes, **2007**

In 1994 when I wanted to migrate up the food chain (getting major contractors for clients), I decided to leverage a relationship I had with another consulting firm. My friend there had some terrific contacts and I told him I felt I needed to reach the CEOs of some key companies to help them maximize the dollar value of their contracts. My friend knew I could help these companies so he suggested I host a dinner party.

With his help (and Rolodex) I held a party for seven to nine people, which included my contact and me, as well as an editor from a government trade publication. The biggest reservation I had about the plan was the venue — I wanted a restaurant with a private dining room complete with our own staff. It was not cheap but it paid off handsomely. There was no agenda or topic for dinner: just general talk.

The very first dinner party ultimately led to high-paying, long-term consulting assignments with several major contractors. My job was simply to keep quiet and let the CEOs mention the event to their CEO friends. Most of the initial invited guests wanted to come back again, and their word of mouth created a backlog of phone messages from administrative assistants, asking when the next dinner was and if their CEO could attend. Many ad agencies

CASE STUDY: MARK AMTOWER

and PR firms in town even offered to pay for the entire dinner if they could be invited!

For two years I hosted one party per month (never for more than nine people) which led to more than $1 million in consulting fees. My visibility in the government contracting community rose rapidly during and after that. To this day, no other marketing or ad agency has my broad access to CEOs at the top contractors. The momentum I gained was astonishing. I went from short-term consulting assignments that were $5,000 to $10,000 to longer-term assignments, some of which were $100,000 a year or more.

To make this work, I recommend an invited guest list only — no substitutes. Spare no expense; go first-class all the way from the venue to the menu and the drinks. Get help inviting the right people to reach the niche you want.

Traditional networking groups meet regularly, typically either weekly or monthly, to enable members to share information about their business. Each member might share a 30-second "infomercial" on themselves and their business, perhaps even mentioning any specials they have available or asking for a particular type of referral. "A good referral for me would be someone who is trying to wrap up their bookkeeping records before the end of the year," an accountant might say in October. Then, the coolest thing happens; those other members actually go out and look for people to send to your business. Of course, you are expected to return the favor.

Some groups are more stringent than others. Some require regular attendance; others figure you come when you can, and you will benefit when you do. There are groups that insist you bring a certain number of referrals to the table each time. While that sounds daunting, just figure that means everyone else is also out there peddling your business while you are trying to find referrals for them. If you are in a group with 30 other networkers, meet your built-in sales staff of 30! Even if you are a sole proprietor you can enjoy the benefits of having multiple people network on your behalf.

One of the more well-known groups is Business Network International, or BNI, one of the world's largest referral organizations. The networking group only allows one person per profession to join a chapter, and each member of that chapter carries your business cards around with them to help promote your company. By developing personal relationships with other business providers, you become a trusted source and new customers are more likely to give your business a try because you come recommended.

Local networking groups are equally useful. Check out your Chamber of Commerce if you are not already a member, and ask the Chamber about area groups that meet regularly to network. Get involved in your trade association or local civic association. All of these are strong ways to integrate yourself with a group of colleagues that may be able to help spread word of mouth about your company. People cannot engage in word of mouth about your company unless they are first aware it exists.

Some online networking groups work just as well without meeting face to face. **www.mommytrackd.com** is a great example of a successful Web-based networking group. Targeted to working moms, the site enables users to offer products and services to help mothers find the balance between work and family. In less than two years, the site has attracted more than 60,000 visitors each month — all of them eager to find ways to make their life easier — and all of them ripe for sharing great stories and input about a business or service they love with other members.

Otherwise, connect with friends, customers, and former coworkers through social networks like **www.LinkedIn.com** and watch how quickly you build a cadre of business referrals. The site helps you find people who can either refer you or give you referrals based on your preferences. It can even help you do high-level networking by connecting you to people you would otherwise have a hard time tracking down. Think of it as the online Kevin Bacon game. What an ingenious way to grow referrals.

Another site, **www.Judysbook.com**, enables people to go online to share opinions about businesses and services. List your company on the site for greater visibility. Encourage your customers to visit the site and write their testimonials. It costs next to nothing and provides small businesses a megaphone to spread word of mouth across the world. You will not even miss the tinny echo.

CASE STUDY: MARY SULLIVAN COOPER

Mommy Mixer, LLC

901 S. Mo-Pac Expressway

Barton Oaks Plaza 1

Suite 300

Austin, Texas 7746

www.mommymixer.com

512-329-2715

Mary Sullivan Cooper — Founding Mama and President

All through college I was babysitting 30 hours a week, and I constantly found that moms and dads who were strangers to me would approach me to help them with child care for their children. Parents have trouble finding great sitters, and at the same time college girls don't have a comfortable, safe means to meet local families to babysit for. I recognized that if this was so

CASE STUDY: MARY SULLIVAN COOPER

in Austin, Texas, it was probably true in many other cities. That inspired me to create MommyMixer, an event that connects two parties that desperately want to meet each other that otherwise may never have met.

I wanted to truly build credibility through using what we call the "Word of Mom." Mom's word of mouth is like word of mouth on steroids...when moms find something they like, they will tell 4 to 10 of their friends. This is something that they will absolutely tell friends about because it is something they believe in.

I stand strong that we will not pay for advertising as I feel you lose a bit of credibility when you pay to promote your business. I want moms to be spreading the buzz for us — creating awareness and establishing MommyMixer as a "real" business that helps both moms and sitters alike.

It is crucial that we make sure that the client is always satisfied and pleased. If a mom is not thrilled with her experience, we work hard to make her experience better or give her money back — no questions asked. We also work hard to provide great experiences for the sitters too. We want to make sure they are going to tell all of their friends what a fabulous service we are providing.

I found out that people love exclusivity! Once our mixers started selling out and were marked "full" on our Web site, I immediately received more demand for more mixers. For some reason, if it is sold out — moms and sitters are even more eager to be a part of it.

I was shocked at how quickly and how far Word of Mom travels. We hold MommyMixers in 16 cities across the U.S. and have requests from across the country. I knew we had generated something really buzz-worthy when the international requests began to roll in from South Africa, Canada, and Europe.

After-Word

- Nothing is more important than your customer. No matter

how innovative your product is, if you do not value your clients, you will not benefit from good word of mouth.

- Customer service hinges on being responsive to your buyers' needs. If you hear about a bad experience, acknowledge it. Do everything in your power to make it right. If you do, people are likely to forgive you. If you do not, they will tell everyone they know.

- Involve your customers as much as you can. Get their advice and input. They will not only feel valued, but they will have a vested interest in seeing your business succeed.

- Bring your customers together to share the energy and positive buzz about your product or service. Good energy breeds good buzz.

- Remind your staff that your customer comes first. Go out of your way to cater to them; you will build strong brand loyalty that translates into great word of mouth.

- Keep in touch with clients. A simple thank-you card, phone call, or email message keeps you in the forefront of their minds.

- Customer evangelists are a potent marketing force. Help cultivate them with VIP clubs, rewards, and incentives.

- Treat your sales staff like gold. Employees are every bit as important to good word of mouth as a great product or service is. A dissatisfied employee can do powerful damage to a budding word-of-mouth campaign.

- Networking groups, whether online or in person, can help you build a strong sales force and customer base.

A Word From the Experts

M. Bryan Freeman is an Atlanta-based entrepreneur who has started Benefits America and Habersham Funding, LLC, both successful businesses. He calls word of mouth a relatively simple, yet powerful, tool that pays phenomenal dividends.

"There are two secrets to networking. One, pay it forward. That's right: Be willing to help other folks without knowing exactly when or how they will reciprocate. It engenders trust and respect and demonstrates that you know that networking is indeed a two-way (at least!) street. People will be all the more willing to help you. Two, thoughtfully select your networking opportunities. For instance, if you envision your perfect client and they are all successful human resources professionals, find organizations where successful HR people gather and go there and network. In other words, don't generalize your networking time if you can zero in with greater specificity on who you need to network with."

— Expert: M. Bryan Freeman

THE B-WORD

MARKETING used to be akin to hunting; decide on your target, pick your weapon, and aim. If you were lucky, you hit a bulls-eye. If you were slightly off the mark, you still may be able to bring your prey down. If you missed completely, there is always another unlucky target to set your sights on.

Nowadays, word-of-mouth marketing is more like farming. It requires sowing the seeds of a good buzz campaign, watering them, watching them grow into a huge harvest, and then sitting down to a big old plate of marketing success. Cultivating the right relationships can help you reap a word-of-mouth campaign to rival any hunting party. And you do not even have to skin your prey.

This chapter examines:

- How to create word of mouth among customers

- The most common mistakes in creating buzz

- How to keep the buzz going

- The best ways to measure and track buzz

BUZZING

Usually, "B-word" has a negative connotation, perhaps linked to an ex-girlfriend or former wife, the monster-in-law who came as a package deal with the latter, or a boss who makes your life worse than the fiery pits of hell. However, when it stands for "buzz," the B-word can make your business B-oom. It has the power to make your product or service B-ecome the next B-ig thing. In this case, the "B-word" has a very positive connotation.

Also, customers can build buzz faster than Superman on speed. They are your ultimate sales force. Nothing can help a business grow quicker than a customer in love with the product. What is really unique is that your customer is not paid for recommendations; he or she truly feels others can benefit from something helpful, and makes it his or her responsibility to see that others know about it.

CREATING BUZZ AMONG CUSTOMERS

Generating a buzz about your business requires a good idea, a sound plan, and quick turnaround. With just a few moves, you can generate strong word of mouth that translates into even stronger sales. Here are four quick steps to effectively create buzz:

Hook 'Em

Just like a great song has a catchy phrase, often called a hook, a great marketing campaign has a hook that will stick in people's minds. How can you creatively increase interest? How can you capture someone's attention long enough to get your message heard?

When Southwest Airlines acquired Morris Air in 1994, the company held a mock marriage in Las Vegas replete with flight attendants as the wedding party and an Elvis impersonator to perform the ceremony. The "wedding announcement" was distributed to media outlets and garnered quite a bit of press, likely far more than a traditional press release.

Crown Royal is another great example. The whiskey maker learned that consumers were using the famous Crown Royal purple bag to create anything from quilts to clothes, so it devised a 2007 contest for the best use of material. The promotion was called "Legends of the Purple Bag." Not only did it garner public attention, but everywhere those entries were sported — from purple golf bags to wedding dresses — resulted in free advertising for the company.

Smaller companies can generate buzz too. One florist I know offers champagne to all prospective brides during their consultation. She purposely books her appointments close together so that the incoming bride-to-be witnesses how much fun everyone is having, which generates even more energy. She also follows up on the one-year anniversary of her client's wedding day, hand-delivering a bottle of champagne for a gift. Most people who are getting married know other people who are getting married — she gets great referrals that way.

Intrigue is a great way to get people's gums flapping. Companies can fuel buzz by keeping some information under wraps, showing a product to a select few, or giving out clues in a marketing campaign without giving away the whole shebang. People are naturally curious to find out more about something that they do not have full access to. It stimulates their natural curiosity and when they are curious, they will talk.

That is not to say you need to withhold all of the good stuff. You need to give the public just enough information to whet their appetite. Then they can muse, wonder, and speculate. And if you have only shared the information with a select few, they feel superior. Now, not only have you appealed to their ego, but you have given them something to share with others, encouraging them to help solve the mystery. That will get the word of mouth flowing.

Whether it is a viral email campaign or a wacky publicity stunt, get people to sit up and take notice. They will talk, guaranteed.

Call to Action

Once you have their attention, get them actively participating. Offer a survey with incentives for those who complete it. Sponsor a contest to get people to enter. The more off the wall your ideas, the better. For example, when a Yoo-hoo delivery truck was stolen in 2003, the CEO of The Geek Factory, a PR company, announced he would give away a two-year supply of Yoo-hoo to help catch those involved. He spent about $500 on a press release, and he sat back to enjoy the swarm of media attention.

Sometimes you just want people to talk about your product or service. After all, talking is the key component to word of mouth, right? If you can get them chatting away with friends and family, you can sip your chocolat-tini and enjoy the free advertising.

Other times, though, you want people to act. You need them to get on board with your marketing efforts in a more involved way. When Cadbury-Schweppes was preparing to relaunch its sports drink called Accelerade, it could scarcely afford to compete in a marketing showdown with Gatorade, so it took a different approach altogether. The company created brand ambassadors by sharing its product with the most respected triathletes, runners, cyclists, coaches, and teams across the United States. It hired six-time Ironman Champion Dave Scott to host performance and nutritional clinics and established Accelerade Aid stations for sports clubs at their local rides, runs, swims, and clinics. Within nine months, Cadbury-Schweppes was enjoying powder sales that were 75 percent higher than the previous year without any change in traditional marketing plans. Word of mouth had accelerated the sports drink beyond expectations and laid the groundwork for a strong product launch.

Netflix made it crystal clear what people needed to do to win some serious cash ($1 million, to be exact). It all had to do with being able to better predict what movies customers will like. Take a look at the copy on their Web site:

> Netflix is all about connecting people to the movies they love. To help customers find those movies, we've developed our world-class movie recommendation system: CinematchSM.... Now there are a lot of interesting alternative approaches to how Cinematch works that we haven't tried.... We're curious whether any of these can beat Cinematch by making better predictions.

In four short sentences, Netflix reinforces their mission ("connecting people to the movies they love"), pat themselves on the back ("our world-class move recommendation system"), appeal to the public's creativity ("a lot of interesting alternative approaches we haven't tried), and finally, entice them to figure out a better way to do it ("curious whether any of these can beat Cinematch"). But here comes the call to action:

So, we thought we'd make a contest of finding the answer. It's "easy" really. We provide you with a lot of anonymous rating data, and a prediction accuracy bar that is 10% better than what Cinematch can do on the same training data set. If you develop a system that we judge most beats that bar on the qualifying test set we provide, you get serious money and the bragging rights. But (and you knew there would be a catch, right?) only if you share your method with us and describe to the world how you did it and why it works.

Netflix tempts the public by calling it "easy" to find a better way to use Cinematch, tempts them with money, appeals to their ego with "bragging rights," and lays out the ground rules: share your method and tell everyone why it works.

Maximize Your Resources

Within your marketing plan, find ways to get the most bang for your buck. Whether that is partnering with another business that can also benefit from (but not compete with) your promotion, or leveraging a friendship with an expert willing to spread the word, make good use of every resource you have — and that includes yourself.

A personal chef and caterer I know of hosts private dinner parties at her home for friends as well as past and future clients. She serves up her culinary expertise, keeping her on past clients' radars while giving prospects a taste of her talent. She hands out catering menus, party checklists, and goodie bags to all who attend. Most of her clients are generated following these events. Talk about a sweet way to cook up some word of mouth!

Even if you are not Betty Crocker, put your resources to work for you. Try making the most of mundane communications. CD Baby is a Portland-based, online record store that sells indie albums. When the company wanted to further its brand it did not turn to traditional advertising. Instead, it used confirmation emails to help it share its satirical style. The email sent to customers who ordered read:

> Your CDs have been gently taken from our CD Baby shelves with sterilized contamination-free gloves and placed onto a satin pillow.
>
> A team of 50 employees inspected your CDs and polished them to make sure they were in the best possible condition before mailing.
>
> Our tracking specialist from Japan lit a candle and a hush fell over the crowd as he put your CDs into the finest gold-lined box that money can buy.
>
> We all had a wonderful celebration afterwards and the whole party marched down the street to the post office where the entire town of Portland waved "Bon Voyage!" to your package, on its way to you, in our private CD Baby jet on this day, [shipping date].
>
> I hope you had a wonderful time shopping at CD Baby. We sure did.
>
> Your picture is on our wall as "Customer of the Year." We're all exhausted but can't wait for you to come back to CDBABY.COM!!
>
> Thank you, thank you, thank you!

What a remarkable way to make a mundane communication sparkle. Granted, this approach may not go over so well among the more serious-minded Jaguar driver or life insurance customer, but the point is that every resource — even something as boring as email confirmations — can become a valuable marketing opportunity. Make the most of every communication with your customers by creating something unique and buzz-worthy. It does not have to take a lot of money; it simply takes a bit of forethought, creativity, and perhaps a touch of tongue-in-cheekiness to maximize your resources.

Create a Theme

Just like a great Halloween costume gets everyone talking, a great theme can generate excitement and buzz. Remember your message, and then craft something that helps deliver it to the press in a media kit. See Chapter 4 for specifics on press releases and other media tools.

Consider what Atlanta-based Duffey Communications did. In 1997, the company redesigned its Web site with a lit Christmas tree, and then issued a press release saying it had "decked the Internet halls." Company analysis reports showed it drove more traffic to the site in December than in any other month that year. It was simple, yet effective.

There are plenty of other easy ways to share your theme. It can be as simple (and free) as crafting one line referencing your theme in your email signature. Or maybe you include some mention of it on your invoices. Keep it visual and visible, and on message. It does you no good to have a theme that cannot reinforce your communications. Otherwise, people remember the theme and forget you. An Internet bank could hire someone to throw dollar bills off a New York skyscraper but it is likely that people will forget who threw it even before they have spent one George Washington.

TOP MISTAKES IN CREATING BUZZ

Remember that word-of-mouth marketing is a step beyond simple word of mouth. People can and will talk, but you need to give them a reason to talk about you and a way to get their voice heard. No matter whether you are a sole proprietor graphic designer or an 18-employee accounting firm, there are several things that can help you manage word of mouth.

- You cannot pay people to say good things. You can offer them incentives or free items or a sneak peek at a new product, but the moment you put a price tag on what their good word of mouth is worth, they have to weigh whether it is worth their word. Word of mouth simply cannot be bought.

- Accepting the status quo is a killer when it comes to good word of mouth. You will need to constantly be innovating. There should always be something evolving or improving your product or service. Each change provides reasons to communicate and interact with people and keep word of mouth flowing.

- A business without a shareable story is like a tree in a rain forest; there is no opportunity to get noticed among all of the others around you. If you are not sure how people would recommend your company or product, you cannot expect them to figure it out on their own. The clearer you can be about what makes your product or service the best, the easier it is for people to help spread the word. Stand out. Tell people what you do and how you do it better. Be the rare jungle lily — but watch out for the killer bees.

Live Buzz Marketing

There are two kinds of live buzz marketing: Peer-to-peer and performer-to-peer.

Peer-to-peer marketing is just as it sounds: ordinary people talking to friends, family, and associates about a product or service they believe in. When marketers get involved to facilitate the discussion, these ordinary Joe Schmoes may be given incentives, samples, or loyalty points to redeem in exchange for their efforts. They are seen as brand ambassadors who are in the know, and as trusted sources who would not steer a friend wrong.

This type of buzz has been around for a while. Some of it is public, where the interaction is transparent. Think about Tupperware, Amway, Mary Kay; these product ambassadors receive discounts or free merchandise in exchange for spreading the word to their family and friends. The pitch is public; everyone knows when they receive an invitation that there will be a product being sold.

Gap created an ambassador program to drive awareness of its new denim fits. The company selected 100 women throughout the country's top ten markets to be brand ambassadors, giving them tools to help share the message with their friends and family. Ambassadors were given a Web site, emails, e-vites, and invitations to their own style party. Gap hosted a private style party for each Ambassador and 30 of her closest friends. After each event, guests were given their favorite pair of jeans, a 20 percent discount, ten friends and family discount cards to pass out, and a gift bag. The ambassador membership card enjoyed a 577 percent redemption rate and the 20 percent discount card for party attendees was redeemed 97 percent of the time. By engaging women on a more personal and emotional level, enabling them to try on the product in a social and relaxed environment, Gap increased overall sales. More importantly, the company shifted women's perception of the styles available at the long-perceived teen-centered retailer.

In 2006, CoffeeCup Software decided to turn happy customers into brand ambassadors to attract new business. The company looked at past purchase patterns to identify candidates with a strong history with the company. These prospects were invited to become ambassadors and were provided T-shirts, business cards, and access to pass-along documents like flyers and posters that they could share with friends. By engaging customers who already were familiar with and supportive of the product, CoffeeCup leveraged a strong and proven sales force to target new consumers. The operation was on the up-and-up; potential customers knew from the start that they were dealing with people affiliated with the company.

Contrast that to the undercover-type of peer-to-peer marketing, where a person has agreed to talk up a product or service without disclosing that the company is providing him or her some type of benefit. For instance, a neighbor hosts a potluck lunch and nosy-pants Norah, the neighborhood snitch, brings dessert: a rich, decadent-looking chocolate mousse. As people ogle it, the mousse-bringer says, "It is actually fat-free and it tastes just like the real thing!" Come to find out, Nosy Norah has been contacted by the mousse-maker and asked to help the company spread the word. She may have received discount coupons or free samples to go out and be a buzz agent. Depending on your point of view (and your opinion of Norah), this is either really underhanded or really smart marketing. It raises the red flag of ethics, again, though — do you want to deceive your friends and family by talking up a product because you are being paid for it? And as a company, are you willing to risk the potential backlash that can occur when people find out they have been duped?

Now take a moment to learn about performer-to-peer marketing. Already, you get the sense that something is make-believe based on the title. Fortunately, it rarely requires the performer to work in tights or makeup. Unfortunately, it also rarely works without some sort of repercussion down the road.

Performer-to-peer works something like this: Trained actors or performers follow a loose script, and they act as ambassadors around the target demographic. This type of marketing is controlled and measured. It is also illegal and immoral but it happens nonetheless. See Chapter 10 for more on ethics in word-of-mouth marketing.

A perfect example of this is Sony when it introduced its Ericsson T68i camera phone in 2002. The company hired teams of undercover buzz agents to pretend to be tourists in cities across the United States. The agents asked people on the street to take their picture using their Sony camera phone and, once they were snapped, would discuss the merits of the phone with the unsuspecting Ansel Adams. Some may label it guerilla, stealth, or undercover marketing. Whatever you call it, it helped Sony raise awareness of its new product.

Freedom Tobacco International, Inc. hired "leaners" to help promote its first line of cigarettes called Legal, which were mainly distributed through Web sites. In 2003, the company paid actresses to smoke the cigarettes in Manhattan bars and nightclubs and to talk up the fledgling brand for several weeks. It also went a step further, offering a free lifetime supply of cigarettes to any celebrity smoker who was willing to be seen puffing on Legals. It was a textbook example of performer-to-peer marketing. Ironically, New York City banned smoking in bars just days after the cigarettes were introduced to the public, and a few months later, the Big Apple became the first state to prohibit its residents to purchase cigarettes online. The timing stunk nearly as much as second-hand smoke, but Freedom Tobacco got its name known, for better or worse.

KEEPING THE BUZZ BUZZING

It sounds simple. Just give them something to talk about and they are off to the races. Word-of-mouth marketing is simple but not quite that easy. If it were, you would not need to read this book. And you do need to read this book. Because creating buzz is one thing; keeping it going is another. If you do not fan the flames of a good word-of-mouth campaign, it dies out too quickly to accomplish all that it can.

Time for a sociology lesson. Do you have your pencil ready? One of the reasons word of mouth stops is what Mark Granovetter referred to as "weak ties." Written in the bell-bottom, peace-sign days of 1973, his paper, called "The Strength of Weak Ties," has since had an influential impact on marketing sociology. The basic premise is that word of mouth will spread quickly through clusters of people who are connected; be it families, churches, or companies. These are people who spend time together, communicate frequently, and typically trust what the other has to say. They have strong social ties. Word typically spreads pretty fast in these clusters — it is a fair assumption that if one person in the group learns something, the others will soon be privy to the information. For instance, when one of the girls on my community swim team tried out for the Olympics and missed it by a couple tenths of a second, everyone on the team — and their parents — knew it within a few hours. It is the old grapevine at work.

The catch comes in that these clusters or groups are separated; almost an island unto themselves. Employees of a company in Wausau, Wisconsin, probably do not do a lot of socializing with the work force of a business in Buffalo. Members of one congregation do not have regular interactions with a church group across the state. While word travels fast in small clusters, getting it to spread out beyond these "islands" is harder. They interact independently of each other. They are the quintessential "weak tie."

That is where bridges come in. You need to get word of mouth to travel from one island to another, so the easiest solution is to build a bridge. Jonathan Frenzen and Kent Nakamoto took Mark Granovetter's work a step further, examining what it takes for a message to jump across a weak tie. They claim you do not need a bridge, per se, but a drawbridge that is raised and lowered (metaphorically, of course) by people depending on the type of message being shared. To determine how messages spread, they took into account factors like the message itself and what effect the message had on the bearer (the phrase "Don't shoot the messenger" comes to mind). They also analyzed the "moral hazard" of sharing the news. In case you are wondering, moral hazard has nothing to do with family values. Think of it as the different ways people behave depending on whether they are insulated from or directly impacted by the message. A man with car insurance may take more risks on the road than the poor soul who does not have any means to protect himself, because the second man knows an accident would wipe him out financially. (Of course, if the first driver switched to Geico, he could also save a bunch of money on his car insurance but that has no bearing on Frenzen and Nakamoto's research.)

Back to the study. Frenzen and Nakamoto used a sale as an example. After all, who does not like a good sale? In one "cluster" they tracked how fast word of a 20-percent-off sale spread. In another group they tracked a bigger discount of 50 to 70 percent. The moral hazard introduced was the number of items available for sale. In one case, there were unlimited numbers available, and in the other there were just a few items available at the discounted price.

The results were not surprising. Word of the deep-discount sale spread farther than when it was only 20 percent off. It was bigger news and more exciting to tell. Word was less likely to jump across weak ties when the moral hazard was high — meaning, when people knew that quantities were limited and feared they may lose out by sharing news of the sale, they were not as quick to tell others. (Seems I am not the only one who is inclined to keep good things for myself.) In short, they were not as likely to lower the drawbridge to other islands.

So, the secret to a successful word-of-mouth campaign is figuring out how to get people to drop those drawbridges. Make it irresistible. Figure out how to capture your consumer's attention with a good message. Analyze the moral hazard that may impact how far and fast the buzz travels. If necessary, plan to help your campaign leap from island to island to keep the word of mouth from sinking in an ocean of weak ties. Do it well and you will be able to afford to do some real island hopping of your own. Class dismissed.

EVENT MARKETING

Nothing gets people talking like the "party of the year," the "wedding of the century," or the "contest of the millennium." The public loves to have something buzz-worthy to chat about and if you create it, your business will be buzzing. It is called event marketing and it is just one more way to create word of mouth for your brand.

Event marketing can mean anything from hosting a booth at a trade show to throwing an invitation-only party. You may consider holding a seminar or a workshop, or getting more visibility simply by sponsoring your local Little League team. It does not have to be anything elaborate, it only needs to showcase your brand somehow.

The point is: Find a way to get your business noticed by a large group of people at the same time. The more people, the better — people tend to create an energy source when they congregate. When they disperse, they take that positive energy with them and share it with the next people they see. If that positive energy is built around your brand, they cannot help but share good WOM.

Malibu Rum used event marketing in its latest campaign, trying to get consumers to see the liquor as something other than a summertime drink. The company hosted Malibu Winter Beach Bashes in 16 cities nationwide, a 10,000 square foot Caribbean beach party replete with indoor volleyball games, cabana lounges with live music, and Malibu Rum-branded flip flops for the guests to wear. The campaign was specifically held in the winter months to help people get past the winter doldrums and dream of summer nights.

Sometimes a great opportunity for event marketing grows out of something much less showy. Consider the Charles Street Boutique, a small hair salon in little La Plata, Maryland (a town famous for a monster of a tornado but little else). The owner, Stacy Scott, was excited about going green by starting a recycling program. She mentioned to me that she was going to buy an ad to let the town know she was recycling. Now, I am all for eco-friendly moves but I failed to see why newspaper readers would care about her environmental moves. Her clients would be happy but how could she spread the word beyond her clientele and into the town at large? So I helped her develop a plan to make a splash with the news. She decided to get her customers involved first-hand by offering a discount to anyone who brought their empty shampoo bottles or hairspray containers. We were on the right track but the drawbridge was still up — we needed to lower it to get her message to extend beyond her clients.

I suggested Stacy work with the town's recycling agency to get the word to spread farther. We named the project "Go Green to Get Green" and her stylists agreed to either dye their hair green (temporarily, of course) or wear green wigs or extensions the day of the event. She put out a press release to the local papers ahead of time to let people know what was planned. The results were fantastic. She gained plenty of exposure, new clients, and a greener small-town boutique. It did not take a huge budget or a marketing guru. Just some time, creativity, and a lot of hair dye to turn other area salons green with envy.

CASE STUDY: SHEL HOROWITZ

Frugal Marketing

16 Barstow Lane

Hadley, MA 01035

www.frugalmarketing.com

www.frugalfun.com

shel@principledprofit.com

413-586-2388 - phone

Shel Horowitz — Author, Principled Profit: Marketing That Puts People First; Grassroots Marketing: Getting Noticed in a Noisy World; Grassroots Marketing for Authors and Publishers

I decided to start my own holiday because it's fun, it is easy to do, and I knew it could lead to media exposure and promotional opportunities.

In October 1999, I geared up the press machine for the first-ever International Frugal Fun Day. When I registered for the holiday it was national, but early publicity generated interest as far away as Japan.

My goal was to get at least five major print media and at least ten radio stations featuring Frugal Fun Day to provide exposure for me and my books. It worked beyond my expectations, driving plenty of word of mouth my way. I saw increased Web traffic and increased reader participation, including a delicious page of Frugal Fun activities all supplied by readers.

It was absurdly easy to do. I requested a form from Chase's Annual Events (www.chases.com) and notified John Kremer (johnkremer@bookmarket.com) that I had an entry to include in Celebrate Today, which is a competitor to Chase's. I hired a company to make phone calls to a media list of my choosing to discuss the holiday and the book.

Creating my own holiday helped me establish myself in the media as a recognized expert and generated interest in my books. It cost next to nothing but bought me a whole lot of word of mouth.

You also keep the buzz going by keeping customers coming back for more. A personal trainer I know of gets 80 percent of her new business from current clients who are happy with her services. She offers a complimentary assessment to new clients at no cost when they sign up for a multisession package. And if an existing client refers someone new, she gives him or her a complimentary session as a way to say thanks. (Now, making me exercise to show your appreciation is akin to giving me a fruitcake; thanks, but no thanks. However, I am sure someone out there appreciates the thought!)

Keeping your clients happy is one of the best ways to keep word of mouth going.

How to Track the B-uzz

There are several ways to measure how much word of mouth you are getting, but there is a catch: there is no sufficient answer on which way is the best, most accurate, or most popular. The Word Of Mouth Marketing Association, the voice of word of mouth, is working on nailing down metrics.

While the association has yet to offer specific tracking devices, it has broken down a word-of-mouth "episode" into four components:

Participants: Creators, senders, and receivers who can be measured on their propensity, demographics, credibility, and reach

- **WOMUnit:** A single unit of marketing-relevant information

- **Action:** What participants do to create, pass along, or respond to a WOMUnit; actions can be measured on velocity, distribution or spread, and source diversity

- **Venue:** The medium or physical location where the communication takes place; venues can be measured on total potential population versus actual audience received

Each episode results in one of the following outcomes:

- **Consumption:** Receiver absorbs information but takes no action

- **Inquiry:** Receiver seeks additional information

- **Conversion:** Receiver completes a desired action

- **Relay:** Receiver redistributes the WOMUnit to another person

- **Recreation:** Receiver creates a new WOMUnit

When it comes to measuring WOMUnits, they can be tracked based on:

- **Topicality:** The degree to which the marketing message is contained in the WOMUnit

- **Timeliness:** Whether the WOMUnit arrives in time to be relevant to a specific campaign

- **Polarity:** The positive versus negative content of the WOMUnit

- **Clarity:** Determines whether the receiver understands the message as the sender intended

- **Depth:** The amount of visual, written, or verbal information included in a WOMUnit presumed to increase message persuasiveness

While the specifics of buzz tracking are being evaluated, there are a few proven methods. One of the easiest ways is to employ a URL that links to your Web site to track results. Be sure you can measure the number of new users, how they found your site (what key words did they use?), and how long they spent browsing. But you also need to know what kind of traffic you had before the campaign started so you have numbers to compare.

Indexing tools can help you follow what is happening in blogs. Begin by narrowing down a list of blogs based on their target audience — find the ones that are most closely in sync with your demo. Then keep an eye on them, and extract meaningful data that relates to your business. Thousands of blogs are written every day, so to follow what people are saying, use analytical software that can capture the information that is pertinent to you. Check out Chapter 7 for more details about blogs.

If you start a viral campaign (read more about viral marketing in Chapter 6), you will need to incorporate a code within the message so that you can assess the performance. You will be able to watch your campaign travel across the world, tracking how long people view your message, and how often it is forwarded.

There are multiple free (yes free, as in "no charge" or "complimentary" or "you-already-know-what-I'm-trying-to-say-so-stop-coming-up-with-examples") monitoring sites that help you keep track of what others are saying about you.

Digg (**www.digg.com**) or Reddit (**www.reddit.com**) are two tools that let you search for any submitted news stories that match your company name (or your competition). You subscribe to RSS feeds and the two sites will automatically notify you when your name comes up in a news story.

Technorati.com does the same thing in social media circles (think of it as a YouTube, Facebook, or MySpace spy).

Google Blog Search (**blogsearch.google.com**) helps you find blogs on your favorite topics. Take it a step further and monitor **www.complaints.com**, which tracks what people write about you on their blogs. And if someone picks up a negative comment about you on complaints.com and links to it? You need **www. blogpulse.com**, which will let you know who is linking to a blog post about you.

Finally, "Book 'em, Danno." You will know if someone bookmarks a Web page that includes a reference to your business thanks to **del.icio.us** (yes, that is the URL too). Billing itself as "social bookmarking," the site lets you keep all of your bookmarks in one place and see what other people are bookmarking. It is great research for you if you need to know what people's favorite sites are.

It is also imperative that you track media placements. Whenever your business is mentioned in an article, blog, or other forum, make note of it on your site. Link to it if possible. Let your viewers know just how much buzz is being generated. The more people see, the more they will talk.

Why is it important to track word of mouth? As George Silverman, author of *The Secrets of Word-of-Mouth Marketing*, writes, "Word of mouth is a live, interactive medium, and depends as much on the questions of the recipients of word of mouth as it does on the senders. In other words, just because an attitude is there, does not mean it will be expressed, or paid attention to."

Tracking word of mouth enables you to know who is saying what, and to whom — all of which are vital elements of any campaign. If people are talking about your product but they are endorsing it to others who are unlikely to need, want, or use it, the buzz does you little good. It dies on the vine. If, however, users tout your brand to people who make up your target audience, Confucius says, "you soon will be toasting your success."

When it comes to researching word of mouth, it would be terrific if you could just ask people, "How would you describe this product to a friend?" and use their response as your basis for buzz. To be honest, that is a very good start. You definitely need to know your talkers understand the product and its advantages. After all, if the message is garbled, word of mouth will not travel very far or very fast.

Nevertheless, face it — understanding the product and accurately describing it is only the first step. Without knowing how her friend answers, or what questions that friend will ask, or what answers your user would give, you just have words, not word-of-mouth marketing.

Focus groups are one of the best methods of researching word of mouth. You can be that proverbial fly on the wall and hear, first-hand, the buzz about your product (wearing wings is optional). Unlike surveys, where you rely on people to accurately remember what they heard, you hear it directly. It is an ideal method of tracking word of mouth.

You also have the chance to hear not only their words but their emotions. What drives their decisions to try your new product?

Does it make them happy to be part of a test group? Do they prefer to wait to try something new until others have given it a trial run? Read between the lines to hear what is not being said. Their emotions, and the unspoken words, carry every bit as much power as what they say about your business.

Some of the things to ask your participants range from product advantages to disadvantages. What would they tell a friend? What objections might they expect? What would they say to overcome those objections? These questions form the basis of word-of-mouth marketing. Knowing the answers enables you to better prepare your campaign to make it as successful as it can be.

Checklist

Before beginning a word-of-mouth campaign, fill in the blanks to these statements. They will help you formulate a stronger, more thought-out program:

- If people only understand one part of our message it should be…

- To spread word of mouth, we will use the following media…

- We will make it easier for conversations about our product to take place by…

- We will track the conversations by…

- The campaign offers a clear call to action by asking people to…

- As an incentive, we will offer…

- To involve brand evangelists, we will…

- To evaluate the results, we will…

By thoughtfully answering these questions prior to launching your buzz-worthy product, you ensure you will stimulate plenty of talk about your company.

After-Word

- Generate buzz about your business by attracting your customers' attention. They will not talk about you if they have never heard about you.

- Get your customers involved with a survey, a contest, or a publicity stunt. When they feel they have invested part of themselves in your business, they will want to share that alliance with others. The result? Word of mouth, of course!

- Use every resource at your disposal to get people talking. Whether it is a wacky email message or a special incentive included on an invoice, make mundane communications something to talk about.

- Word of mouth spreads quickly through connected groups like neighborhoods, churches, and workplaces. Beyond those groups, it is easy for buzz to fizzle out faster than an open bottle of soda. To spark word of mouth for your business, develop a great product, a strong message, and an unstoppable way to get those groups connected and talking among themselves and other enclaves.

- Tracking buzz is imperative in a word-of-mouth campaign.

After all, how will you know if your efforts are successful if you do not keep track of how they spread?

- Focus groups are a great way to know what people are saying about you. If your message is getting garbled, word of mouth may not be helping you as much as it should.

- Develop a clear set of goals and strategies before you start your campaign. Follow the steps — no shortcuts — to ensure that you will successfully accomplish your mission to build plenty of word of mouth.

A Word From the Experts

Paul Rand is the president and CEO of Zócalo Group and former global chief development officer of Ketchum. He is also the co-chair of the Word of Mouth Marketing Association.

"Find people that have the ability to refer and recommend others. They may or may not be direct buyers of the service. If you are in a business that appeals to homeowners, reach out to bankers, real estate agents, brokers. Find out who is the most popular in that community and hook up with them. Share with them what you do and ask their advice on how they can help you grow."

— Expert Paul Rand

VIRTUAL WORDS

WORD of mouth has been around since the days of the dinosaurs, when the velociraptors ran around and told their buddies where they could find a great buffet of fresh Brachiosaurus butt. (I am not certain, but rumor has it, it tastes like chicken.)

Unlike our dinosaur friends, word of mouth has evolved over the ages. With the advent of the World Wide Web, it has morphed into something so powerful it could tackle a T-Rex. Messages can spread farther, faster, and more pervasively than ever before, all thanks to the Internet. While e-mail might have been the driving factor in the early days of online WOM, today there is a veritable smorgasbord of ways to reach an audience and generate buzz. And you do not even have to worry about carnivores devouring your hard work.

This chapter examines:

- Live buzz marketing

- Internet marketing

- Online press releases

- Discussion forums and boards

- Affiliate marketing

WORLD **W**IDE **W**EB OF **M**OUTH

Information age, shminformation age. Many are so tired of hearing that term that it is easy to forget what an incredible thing this era is. Word spreads like wildfire — the world tunes in to watch O.J. Simpson being chased by police, news of the latest celebrity faux pas hits water coolers like water balloons at a frat party, and within minutes of "The Sopranos" finale, the Internet is bogged down by those who had to discuss whether they loved or hated the ending. The public is connected at so many levels by so many devices it is hard to become unplugged. This, if you are seeking to grow a successful WOMM campaign, is a remarkable thing.

Depending on what kind of campaign you are trying to start, virtual marketing can go a long way toward ensuring that the world at large (or at least the city of Toledo) will be introduced to your product or service. Of course, once they are familiar with it, they will fall in love with it just like you did, and you are off and running.

INTERNET **M**ARKETING

Remember life before the Internet? Me neither. It is amazing that we have come to rely so heavily on something so relatively new, but online marketing is one of the quickest and most expansive (not expensive) ways to generate serious word of mouth. However, that is not to say the 'Net is the ultimate marketing tool.

The benefits of Internet marketing are as clear as they are diverse. When it comes to buzz marketing, nothing tops the Web for getting the word out quickly, widely, and inexpensively. Consumers can access information and purchase products or services 24 hours a day, 7 days a week from the comfort of their own home or by clicking a few buttons on their Web-based mobile phone. Companies save money by marketing online, requiring fewer salespeople and store locations. In addition, they can market to a world-wide audience instead of attracting customers to a store front.

Check it out: When Heinz Ketchup launched its campaign to get fans to create its next commercial (thereby saving themselves the cost of creating an ad), it created the "Top This TV Challenge." More than 4,000 viewers submitted their video entries on **www.topthistv.com**, and then the company asked America to log on and choose a winner. The first campaign in August 2007 was so successful that the company launched a second one a few months later.

Despite the numerous benefits, there are a few drawbacks to online marketing. Not all consumers are Web-savvy, meaning marketers may miss a large segment of the population. Seventy-one percent of American households have an Internet connection. That is a lot of people, but it still leaves out almost 30 percent of the United States. Even those that are comfortable on the keyboard may not have a fast-enough connection or appropriate memory space to download or view a complicated Web page. And one obstacle that can never be overcome is the inability for the consumer to handle a product before buying; they will never be able to try on that chic pair of jeans or smell the tantalizing aroma of freshly ground coffee beans while shopping online.

If you are willing to overlook the drawbacks and forge ahead in the big, bad Internet world, you will find a willing and able audience to spread word of mouth about your company. Good Web marketing gets traffic to your site, makes sales, and reinforces your company's brand. Successfully navigating the 'Net to generate buzz requires a few ground rules, though.

Get a Good Domain Name

Make it memorable. Make it easy to spell. And make it yours— do not fall in love with a domain name that is already taken. Check **www.uspto.gov** to be certain yours is not trademarked by someone else. Whenever possible, make the domain name relate to your business name so your brand is reinforced every chance you get. You may even consider choosing two domain names: one that coincides with your business name and one for your main product name. Both can point to different pages of the same Web site. That way, customers who only know your product's name can find you easily, as can those who know your company's name. Wondering whether to keep your maiden name or not? The jury is still out on whether longer domain names should contain hyphens. Some people think it makes them easier to read; others argue that it is too hard to remember those pesky dashes.

Build Your Web Site, and They Will Come

But only if it is professional looking and easy to navigate. Forget the Flash intro and talking anime salesperson. Keep it simple so viewers can focus on your content. And speaking of focus, stick with a simple background with contrasting text to make it easy to read. Remember to add search capabilities on your site so visitors can quickly find exactly what they want to see.

Size Sometimes Matters

You may be considering launching a word-of-mouth program that is a completely separate entity than your regular product or service. One of the best ways to showcase it is on a microsite, also called a minisite or a Weblet. Basically, in Austin Powers speak, that means it is the "Mini Me" of your primary Web site. Microsites can be completely separate from your main site or linked to it, although they usually have a main landing page with a separate URL.

Because they can focus on something either temporary or ancillary to your primary site, microsites may contain different keywords that enable greater search engine results. Ding! Ding! Ding! More people can find you more efficiently. See? Small can be good.

Money Management International put that theory to the test. The nonprofit organization seeks to help consumers understand more about using finances wisely. (I will likely never be their poster child.) Holidays are a time that spending is out of control for many people so the organization created a holiday-themed microsite called **regiftable.com**.

The basic message was that, if done correctly, re-gifting may be a suitable alternative to buying new presents and can corral out-of-control spending. (Before you jump on your high horse and stop reading this book, simmer down. You know you secretly wanted to pass that chocolate fondue set on to someone else.) Now, there may never be a suitable situation for re-gifting fruitcake, but Money Management International wanted to encourage word of mouth both online and off to spread the idea of smart spending habits. The microsite enabled visitors to share their re-gifting stories to help generate ideas for gift giving, as well as Re-gifting 101 (bottles of wine are apparently only good to re-gift as long as they are still unopened). It also featured interactive elements such as the ability to create personalized gift certificates as an alternative to purchasing gifts. Within the one-month campaign, regiftable.com generated nearly 600 media exposures including mentions on CNN, Associated Press, and in newspapers like *The New York Times* and *The Wall Street Journal*. That coverage translated into more than 230 million media impressions. The site attracted nearly 100,000 visitors. Not bad for a site pushing used but uneaten fruitcake.

Optimize Your Site for Search Engines

Outside of the marketing realm, that phrase may sound like something heard in an episode of *Star Trek*. I can hear it now: "Mr. Spock, optimize the site for search engines." "Optimizing now, Captain." However, it is one of the most crucial elements of marketing and if you have not already done it, make it priority number one. When you set up your Web site, make it "friendly" to different search engines like Google and Yahoo! Use title tags and keywords to make the search engines index your site more efficiently, which ultimately means your site gets a better ranking among search results, which drives more traffic your way. Look out! I think there is a Romulan ship headed right for you.

Also, rankings are more key than key words for searches. When HGTV wanted to promote its new show called *Living With Ed*, a reality show about Ed Begley Jr., the network discovered a slight problem: A quick search on the 'Net resulted in numerous listings discussing life with erectile dysfunction ("ED"). Instead of generating awareness, increasing site traffic, and inspiring viewers to tune in, the network was being confused with a sexual condition. To provide HGTV a better ranking in search results, they turned to bloggers, encouraging them to write reviews of the program. The fresh new content would land the show higher in search results and stimulate more word of mouth. In addition, the bloggers linked back to **www.HGTV.com** which drove more traffic to the site.

PLANT THE SEEDS

Your Web site is the hub for customers and prospects to find out more about your business; however, it would be bad business to sit back and wait for traffic to come to you. You need to get out there and plant seeds of interest all over the World Wide Web. This includes creating a profile on social networking sites like LinkedIn, Twitter, Facebook, and Flickr (read more on social networking in Chapter 9). Each profile links back to your Web site. Beyond that, become actively engaged in blogs, product reviews, and anything else where you can drop a link to your site. You have planted the seeds; now enjoy watching them come to fruition through buzz and sales.

GEOTARGETING IS NOT JUST FOR ROCK HUNTERS

It will not do you any good to advertise to people in Thailand if your company can only do business in Texas. That is where geotargeting comes in. It is a feature that lets you target your Internet ads to specific countries and languages when you are creating a new AdWords campaign. For instance, you select the country, region, and the languages in which your ad will appear. Your ad will only be visible to users who live in those areas and who have selected the same language you chose.

MAKE YOUR LANDING PAGES USER-FRIENDLY

People are too busy to take time on long, complicated forms. It is a big turnoff — worse than toe jam, if you can believe it. So when a potential customer gets to your site, be wary of asking too many questions. Keep your forms short and sweet. All you really need to know in the beginning is someone's contact information, so ask for their e-mail, name, and phone number. You can include a line about what product or service they are interested in, but this is not the time to ask them how they heard about you, or how many descendants removed they are from the Pilgrims. Those tidbits of information can wait.

GOLDILOCKS WAS HERE

Know who has been visiting your site and how they found it. There are amazing search metrics available to provide you information on who has clicked on — or through — your site. You can easily learn how many hits per day your site is attracting, what keywords visitors used to find you, and how long they stayed on a page. Your webmaster should be able to compile a report on a regular basis using tools like Visual Sciences, Google Analytics, or ClickTracks. You can glean information on just about anything (except maybe what a visitor ate for breakfast that day) and all of it is important in tracking how and where word of mouth is spreading.

LET THE CONSUMER DO THE WORK

As opposed to having a salesperson breathing down their neck the moment they cross the threshold of a store, consumers love to do their own research online. They will sell themselves on products by checking out detailed specs and customer reviews. And when they do, they are more likely to share their own opinion with others, spreading word of mouth about your business for you.

Beyond the research, customers are becoming more involved in the marketing efforts of many companies, helping to develop marketing strategies and determine where a campaign goes. You read about the growth of customer-generated marketing (CGM) in Chapter 1. What follows are a few examples of how consumers are dictating marketing campaigns.

Visit the Geico Caveman Crib (**www.cavemanscrib.com**) and you have the chance to help write the ongoing story line with the Geico marketing team. That is right — you can determine what those wacky, evolution-challenged hairballs will do next, including helping them pick out clothes ("Is this a chick shirt or what?"), grabbing a sneak peek at the "Musings of a Caveman" blog, or playing darts with a picture of the company's gecko as the bulls-eye.

Neutrogena wanted to build brand awareness about its line of men's grooming products. The company got a chin up on its competition by using a nontraditional marketing approach, letting CGM work its magic. Neutrogena engaged students on college campuses nationwide, partnering with them to develop the "Undercover Hotties" promotion. Launched on the microsite **www.shavehisface.com**, students could nominate others on campus who they thought would be irresistible if only they shaved their facial hair. Brand ambassadors at each school were taught about Neutrogena and given effective marketing tactics to help the promotion. They used flyers, posters, online networking, and campus events to spread the word, and boy, did it work! The microsite logged nearly 15,000 unique visitors in one month, with more than 1,000 pictures of hairy students uploaded — all of it generated by consumers. The top 30 winners from each campus took part in a Neutrogena shave clinic to showcase the brand and its results. By letting students take the reins instead of marketing professionals, the campaign generated increased awareness and sales. There is no word yet on whether the company is considering a similar promotion for a collection of ladies' bikini line products.

More and more companies are turning to CGM to help their word-of-mouth campaigns. Obviously, it is a cost-effective method of creating marketing materials. It also — and this is key — gives people a sense of being closer to a brand. Beyond that, it generates great buzz as homegrown videos are being watched more and more. Accustream iMedia Research reported in 2007 that user-generated videos were viewed 22 billion (yes, billion with a "b") times world-wide. That figure is up 70 percent over 2006. Anything with that kind of growth is either malignant or becoming mainstream in a big way.

Even the Super Bowl, where advertisers pay out the wazoo for air time, now features "You"-themed ads. In 2007, Doritos invited musicians to submit original songs on its MySpace page, which viewers could then vote on. The winning song aired as a 60-second music video during the big game. Not a bad way to get national exposure. Of course, the winner would forever be known as "all that and a bag of chips."

Think of CGM as a new twist on Halloween — as a consumer, you do the trick, and marketers get the treat: a whole lot of loyal customers and even bigger buzz.

ONLINE PRESS RELEASES

A search engine–optimized press release can garner attention like nobody's business, increase sales, enhance your image, and, yes, generate buzz. It is one of the most effective ways to reach a large number of influencers, and it is a credible form of advertising that sends your message soaring across the Internet like birds in the late October skies. It also creates the perception that your brand is omnipotent because your release will be seen in everything from e-mails to RSS feeds. Plus, it does not have to cost you an arm and a leg. In many cases, you can send an online press release for free.

Ensuring that your press release is picked up requires following a few simple rules and some good common sense:

1. The information has to be newsworthy. This is not an ad. That is why it is called a "press" release. Aptly named, eh?

2. Begin with a short description of your news, and then say who announced it. It may sound counter intuitive but you need to hook your reader into reading more.

3. That said, the first dozen or so words of your release are crucial. Make every one of them count. There is no room for fluff here.

4. The information has to be newsworthy.

5. Just the facts and nothing but the facts. This is not the place for you to showcase your immense vocabulary or to see how many different ways there are to say "great."

6. The information has to be newsworthy.

7.   Contact information is critical. Provide a contact name and give every possible phone, fax, and locker combination number for people to reach you.

8.   The information has to be newsworthy.

You may have noticed some duplication in the above list. There is a good reason for that. If you do not have something worth writing about, do not send a press release. Not only will you be wasting time and resources on something that will not net you anything, but you will also tick off the journalists who took the time to read it and damage your chances at catching their attention when you really do have something to share. There is nothing to be gained by sending out a premature press release (except some nice alliteration).

Once your release is written, do some research on news services. Find one that specializes in reaching your target audience. Many of them offer writing services to help you craft the perfect press release, so if you are not satisfied with your efforts, you have a helping hand. All of them have requirements for submissions, so familiarize yourself with their methods of formatting, whether it is a preset template or a form. Nothing says you have to rely on one service; submit your release to several, and maximize your chances for exposure. Just like options in a candy store, the more choices you have, the merrier you will be.

Keywords are a key component (see how well they are named?) to successful online press releases. You can optimize your press release by including top keywords a couple of times, in both the headline and the text of your piece. Add a few more keywords throughout the body of the release but be careful not to overdo it. And remember to check in to whether your news service allows you to include an embedded link within the text — many do and it is a powerful way to link back to your Web site.

Be sure to include functions that enable readers to easily forward your release as well as print it out for future reference. Both options ensure that your release enjoys a longer Web life than it might otherwise have. The buttons "print PDF" and "e-mail this link" can go a long way toward spreading word of mouth. Without them, your release is much more likely to wither on the vine than blossom into buzz.

After you have submitted to your news service, track your release. Google and Yahoo! can help you monitor who has found your news online. Keep an eye on your zsite to see how much your traffic increases. This is the only time I can imagine where "rush hour" is truly enjoyable — and you are not even subjected to the thumping sounds of a jacked-up bass system in the vehicle next to you.

DISCUSSION FORUMS AND BOARDS

Discussion boards are the ideal place to find, leave, and track buzz about your business. They are created specifically to let people "talk" to one another without sales or marketing getting in the way, clouding any judgment, or inspiring sales. They are honest reflections of how people feel about a product or service.

Think about it: You are giving customers (and potential customers) a place where they can talk about your products all the time. They can share passion about your industry and help generate excitement around your business. In some cases, posts are anonymous (which has the potential to involve some underhandedness) but in many cases, people freely post their true opinions along with their real names or e-mails.

Now, not all companies would really need to create a discussion forum or board. Some are simply too narrowly focused to warrant this type of tool and may do better creating a blog instead (see Chapter 7 for more on blogging). For instance, how much enthusiasm or passion can you generate to discuss an alarm company? Or a plumber? No matter how top-notch their service is, it is hard to imagine that people would be breathlessly logging on to express their observations about the latest tools in those industries. There are, though, some businesses that can benefit from a discussion board. They can be summed up in one thought: they fill an emotional void.

For example, people are passionate about politics, religion, and parenthood. They get riled up over taxes, corporal punishment, and whether to legalize marijuana. Check out any discussion board that contains the phrase "animal cruelty" or "potty training" (not that those two subjects go together in any way!). You will see that they are rife with posts from people who cannot help but share their opinion. Once one opinion is posted, others that support it or differ from it are sure to follow, creating a public dialogue.

If your business does not encompass one of the above topics, you can still consider a discussion board — you just have to find your place within the hot-button issues. Give people a place to vent and respond, and help stir up some more passion in your industry. When folks are talking about your industry in general, it is easier to get them talking about your business specifically. Do I hear some word of mouth starting up?

AFFILIATE MARKETING

What if you found a way to either make more money thanks to an advertiser or advertise and make more money? Affiliate marketing is one often-overlooked avenue to buzz building.

The gist is this: You build a great Web site that attracts plenty of visitors. Say you are a realtor with a top-notch Web site filled with great information. Sally Lou is surfing and comes across your site. As she is reading an article on the best way to increase her home's value, Sally Lou sees an ad that catches her eye. It is for a mortgage company. She clicks on it and fills in some information to get a basic rate quote. Bam! You just earned a cool $75 commission for providing a lead to the mortgage company. Sally Lou is thrilled with the deal she found on your site and talks about both the great information she got on your site and the incredible rate she found. It is word of mouth, working its magic.

There is another way that affiliate marketing can help you. Say that you are the mortgage company in the above example. You pay someone to link to you on their Web site and you generate qualified lead after qualified lead without cold calling. Sure, you are paying a bit more for word of mouth this way, but you are also reaping the benefits of smart marketing while minimizing your costs to showcase your business.

The top money-making affiliates include poker sites, mortgage sites, and education-related providers. That does not mean you are limited to affiliating with those segments, however. Find a natural fit between you and another type of business in your general industry and see if affiliate marketing can help you build a little buzz.

Words to the wise: The most effective affiliate marketing contains photos. If you are advertising on someone else's site, include a picture of your product, your company logo, or something that catch a reader's attention.

After-Word

- Live buzz marketing can take two forms: peer-to-peer and performer-to-peer. Both have their places, as long as they are done ethically.

- Internet marketing holds tremendous value in a word-of-mouth campaign but it cannot compensate for those who do not have access to the Web or who simply must try on a pair of jeans before buying them.

- A dynamic Web site is key. It should be aptly named, easily navigated, and professional looking.

- Utilize search metrics to know who has visited your Web site and how they stumbled onto it. It is imperative that you know how and where your word of mouth is working.

- Online press releases can reach an enormous amount of influencers. Be sure they are newsworthy, factual, and concise. They should contain keywords to help readers find you, as well as functions that enable others to forward and print your release.

- Discussion boards and forums are a great way to help build word of mouth about an industry, and specifically, your business. Not all products or services warrant discussion boards, though; they work best for businesses that can link to popular topics.

- Affiliate marketing is a relatively inexpensive way to

either bring in more clients or more money, depending on how you approach it. Regardless of whether you provide the site or the service that advertises on one, you are likely to help generate more discussion about your business.

A Word From the Experts

Missy Cohen-Fyffe created the Clean Shopper, a shopping cart cover to protect babies from germs. She has grown it into a $2 million business.

"I first conducted a PR campaign, which didn't cost my company a dime. This consists of writing and issuing press releases. I did make the packages clever, and that's key. And I specifically targeted journalists at national parenting publications who specifically wrote about new products. I sent the release inside a miniature shopping cart ($12) and put my miniature Clean Shopper in the front seating area. I put the real, packaged, Clean Shopper in the basket portion of the cart and mailed it off via UPS Ground in a box. The product was picked up in the national media and that generated significant sales which led to increased word-of-mouth. When my 'news' was no longer 'new' (in other words, we had been written about significantly in the press, and I had appeared on *Good Morning America*, and other morning programs), that's when I started actually 'paying' for advertising."

— Expert Missy Cohen-Fyffe

5

ALL THE WORLD'S A STAGE

THERE are stages of a word-of-mouth campaign, just as there are stages to the marketing strategies of old. It used to be that businesses only cared about increasing the number of customers, the average transaction amount, and the frequency of purchases. Increasing any one of those factors meant linear growth. Increasing all three of them meant geometric growth. Since math was never my strong suit, I was never much of a fan of the old way of doing things. (The words "linear" and "geometric" simply reminded me too strongly of Mr. Foil, my eighth-grade math teacher with the weirdest combover you ever saw. He combed his hair into an infinity symbol on his head. No kidding!)

I much prefer today's word-of-mouth marketing stages, which involve so much more interaction with people. WOMM is not simply based on people going out and selling your business. Instead, it requires strategic messaging, customer nurturing, and careful tracking to see where all the buzz is going. When done correctly, it results in an infinite amount of good word of mouth for your brand. See? I did learn something from Mr. Foil, after all.

This chapter covers:

- Developing a strong message

- Finding the right people

- Hearing what the public has to say

- Using strategies to create buzz

- Tracking word of mouth

DEVELOPING A CAMPAIGN

It would be terrific if word-of-mouth marketing were really as simple as Mary telling her family and friends about your business, and it suddenly was moving faster than a roller coaster at Disney World (hopefully without the annoying tune of "It's a Small World, After All"). Unfortunately, it takes more planning, more management, and more measurement than that. Remember, word of mouth has been around forever. Word-of-mouth marketing is a fairly new phenomenon but as we have already seen, it is potent in its potential to get your business noticed.

Like any successful marketing campaign, there are phases to creating buzz. In fact, there are five basic stages to developing a word-of-mouth marketing campaign.

1. Craft your message

2. Target your talkers

3. Listen up

4. Haven't you heard?

5. Tracking devices

Now we get to the heart of word-of-mouth marketing. It is all about what you hear and how you hear it — or conversely, what you say and how you say it. Remember my son who wants to be Wonder Boy when he grows up? He has not perfected the flying part yet but I am more concerned about his hearing. While I was talking with my husband on the phone one day, I mentioned I was making beef stew for dinner that night. My son piped up, "Bee stew? Yuck! I am not eating any bees!" After I finished laughing I told him that I had said "beef." But when I then explained that I was also making dumplings we had a real crisis of communication. My son heard "Dumb things." Thus, a perfectly good comfort food was reduced to a disgusting-sounding concoction of stingers and stupidity.

And therein is a perfect example of why having a crystal-clear message that is easy to convey — and understand — is crucial.

Craft Your Message

The easiest way to start developing your message is the old elevator example. What do you say when you are in an elevator and someone asks, "What does your company do?" You have got about 30 seconds (maybe 45 seconds if you are both headed to the top of the Chrysler Building) to answer. But in that time you have your work cut out for you.

Your message needs to do more than answer the question. It needs to excite, to intrigue, and to attract. It should grab your prospect's attention, convey why they should trust you and why they should do business with you over any competitor. That is a lot of ground to cover in a 30-second elevator ride.

Think about the problems your target audience experiences. It will help you connect with them on an emotional level. Then think about how your product or service helps them. That is the key to reaching people — conveying to them that you have something they need or want.

You also need your message to be as clear as water. Positive word of mouth that is inaccurate can be every bit as damaging as negative buzz (which you will read more about in Chapter 11). Say you operate the city's largest plant nursery and you mention it on the elevator one day. You say something about how you cannot believe the growth at Nancy's Nursery. Cousin Cindy overhears and gets the false idea that you run a child-care center. She is all set to enroll her four little darlings in a part-time daycare program, until she calls and finds out that you change plant soil, not Pampers, and that "greenhouse" is not just another term for the timeout corner. Cindy may be aggravated just because she misunderstood. While it is no fault of yours, the sheer frustration she feels may be enough for her to bad mouth you to the other mothers in her kid's play group. Suddenly, you have created negative publicity by not being crystal clear about what your company does. Be sure your message is easy to understand and not misunderstood.

Be ready to prove to your prospect that your business is the answer to their problem. Explain how they can benefit from your product or service, and be able to communicate how you can serve them better than a competitor. This is your own personal infomercial (without the annoying, overly cheerful operator who is standing by to take my call). Remember, the fun in the elevator lasts only 30 seconds, but in word-of-mouth marketing you have got a bit more time — though not much — to share your solution. Remember your elementary school rule and use your time wisely. It will pay off.

Your message should:

- Contain facts about your product or service

- Rally the troops in a strong call to action

- Avoid speculation or innuendo

- Be clear and concise without using confusing terms or jargon

Target Your Talkers

With a good product and a strong message in hand, you need to find someone to share it. You cannot build a good word-of-mouth campaign without a great product, but buzz actually begins with talkers. People who like to talk are the best form of marketing you will ever have. Wait a minute. Back up. People who like your product and like to talk are the best source of marketing. I have known several Chatty Cathys who may not translate into great brand ambassadors because they do not know how to talk about something other than themselves, but that is beside the point.

Talkers are fairly easy to pinpoint and they are the impetus behind your buzz. If you can hook up with some of them, you are well on your way to word-of-mouth nirvana. Where do you find them?

They are the customers who fill out your comment cards or write letters of praise. They are the people who email, call, or text you to tell you that your product or service is tops. They blog about you or review your product online and in forums. They are the ones who frequent your business again and again. Next time they do that, snag them and thank them for their business. There is no need to schmooze them, because that could come across as insincere, but you need to let them know you appreciate their support. Not only does it make them feel good but they feel more connected to your company than the average customer. Foster that connection with everything you have got. Believe me; it will pay big dividends down the buzz road.

You do not have to wait for the talkers to come to you; it is equally important that you approach them. Engage potential talkers with a call to action they cannot refuse. Run a contest, create a survey, and find a way to get them engaged with your brand. Once a customer has participated in something positive that is related to your organization, you are in a better position to rev them up as a brand ambassador.

Look for people who are online. Those who strongly believe in a brand are quite likely to create a Web site to share their passion. Find those people. Visit Web sites dedicated to your competition. You may learn a few things in addition to trying to persuade a competitor's fan to give your product a try. Be above-board, however; anytime you are trying to attract a new customer, let them know who you are and who you are affiliated with.

Look for people who are online. Oh, did that sound redundant after the last paragraph? That is because you want to seek out those who are online and buzzing about your business. If someone takes the time to write about you, they must feel strongly about your product or service. Capitalize on that. Respond to their post with a thank you and offer them some sort of incentive to be more involved in your business. Or if it is a negative post, work on appeasing them. Do not just ignore them and hope they will go away. They will not. Read more about that in Chapter 11.

When you have found your talkers, I.D. them. No, I do not mean give them a code name. I mean give them some free stuff. Hand out logo bags, hats, or beach towels. Give them shirts and jackets and aprons. I never met anyone who did not like free stuff, and if the free item happened to bear the logo of a company they liked, all the better. It is free advertising for you (well, free except for the cost of the item, but surely you get my point) and makes them feel special and valued. Oh, and clothed.

CASE STUDY: M. BRYAN FREEMAN

Habersham Funding, LLC

Building 11, Piedmont Center

3495 Piedmont Road NE, Suite 910

Atlanta, GA 30305-1755

www.habershamfunding.com

bfreeman@habershamfunding.com

404-233-8275 - phone

M. Bryan Freeman - President

Viral messaging, in its loosest definition, has been key to word-of-mouth marketing for my business ventures. Simply put, I've taken care to identify folks who wanted or needed to know about the work I was doing, and who are in a position to themselves share such information. I communicated with them about what I was doing. In turn, they became ambassadors for me.

I didn't really have an initial, formalized concept for a buzz campaign when I started my business doing life settlements. Rather, I just did what I knew how to do: Spread the word about what I was doing, how I could help people through my business, and how they might be able to help me.

Word-of-mouth marketing need not be complicated. In the beginning, I had little or no marketing budget, but a great enthusiasm for my work, so I got out and talked to people and pressed the flesh, meeting as many people as I could.

CASE STUDY: M. BRYAN FREEMAN

We are actively involved in our industry and the industry we serve. We attend industry meetings; we are always willing to talk to any and every group that wants to know about our work. As a result, we get a great deal of "earned media" exposure; people recognize us as an industry leader and as experts and they write about us. Our word of mouth happens very genuinely.

Making wise choices is an important facet in word of mouth. That includes knowing when not to pursue an opportunity for word-of-mouth exposure. You have to choose your battles or you can spend all of your time marketing what you do, and none of the time doing the work you love.

Listen Up

I have heard that for every positive letter or comment you get, you will receive ten negative ones. Not that there are more negative people out there, but the dissatisfied ones are more likely to pipe up. So, if you get someone with something good to say, acknowledge it. My mom loves to tell the story of a box of chocolates she received (and she is no Forrest Gump, believe me). They are from a little company called Purity, based in upstate New York, and she swears they are the best chocolates she has ever had. She took the time to write and tell them so, and they wrote back! Not a stilted company response but a little handwritten note written on the top half of a card. She got such a kick out of the fact that a real person responded that she told a bunch more people about the candy — free marketing for Purity. And now I have told you. That is some sweet word-of-mouth marketing that cost someone five minutes and the price of a stamp.

Matt Galloway, an independent blogger, thought it prudent to have a central place where people could call and compliment or complain about a company, so he started Buzz-o-Phone as a way to explore word of mouth. The goal was to encourage people to call a toll-free number to collect opinions about a product, service, brand, or company. Callers had two minutes to rant about any of the above, and then Galloway selected the best ones and made them available via podcast so that people could hear what others were saying.

Orbitz listened to feedback showing that customers value insight from other customers. As a result, that led the company to launch a user-generated tip Web site that offers real-time updates from travelers. Topics include weather information, how long fliers will wait in line at security checkpoints, the best place to get an airport snack, and the latest air traffic updates, to name just a few. It is a winning combination in several ways: travelers trust that the information they are getting is current, reliable, and unbiased; airports, airlines, and other travel services get the chance to hear what travelers are saying about their products and services; and the company is enjoying increased traffic at its Web site, all while promoting the Orbitz brand.

More often than not, customer reviews are positive. In fact, 87 percent of reviews are generally positive in tone, according to one 2007 study. Respondents gave most product and service reviews an average of 4.3 out of a possible score of 5. Therefore, give people a chance to praise you and enjoy the positive word of mouth that results. Regardless of whether they are saying good things or bad, you need to let consumers have their say.

Then it is up to you to respond. Cadbury did, after Facebook users spoke up and demanded the candy-maker bring back a chocolate bar called Wispa. Using a digital petition, nearly 14,000 Facebook users demanded that the company reintroduce the candy bar. Some went so far as to post old TV commercials for the discontinued product. Cadbury listened, bringing back the candy bar. Not only did the company give consumers a good sugar high, it also leveraged some great word of mouth by listening to what candy lovers had to say.

FOX listened when its viewers talked about its show "Family Guy." After two years, the network pulled the plug on the show, instead concentrating on launching a word-of-mouth campaign to promote the show's DVD. Fans glommed onto the opportunity, building Web sites and successfully recruiting others to convince network execs to bring the show back on the air.

Think of it this way: You would probably never walk into a public place and just start talking, assuming everyone would want to listen to what you have to say. Rather, you would listen to the conversations around you, and if you had something to add, you would chime in. The same goes for marketing. Resist the urge to spout out about your product until you know what page your audience is on. When the time is right, bring your business into the conversation. Believe me, it will feel a lot more natural and be a lot more successful.

Haven't You Heard?

There are so many great ways to get your business on people's radars. You truly are limited only by your imagination. Whether you utilize clever publicity stunts or fervent fans, you can help get the word out there in a way that is above-board and attention-grabbing.

Fan Clubs

Want to know a not-so-well-kept secret? People like to feel like they belong. Help them belong to your business by making them feel special. It can be as easy as creating a fan club or selling logo merchandise. When Saturn first came on the scene, they had the tagline, "A different kind of company. A different kind of car." They took and hung up pictures of new car owners standing next to their new jalopies and people ate it up. They hosted annual homecoming events at their manufacturing plant in Spring Hill, Tennessee, and people from around the country came just because they were invited. Now, I do not know about you but I do not crave going to parties where I will not know anyone, but Saturn fans felt like part of a great big family and drove thousands of miles to meet other "family" members.

Harley-Davidson is another company that has managed to make its customers feel like part of a special group. The mother of all motorcycle companies created the Harley Owners Group in 1983 as a way for customers to share their passion for their machines. More than 20 years later, there are more than one million people in 1,200 local HOG chapters worldwide. There was a time when being called a hog would offend some people, but now the title is considered a badge of honor — only in America.

In early 2007, the Baltimore Ravens football team launched a free, woman-only fan club called Purple. In less than one year, the club had 3,500 members sign up to receive inside information on the team, exclusive offers for ladies' team jewelry and apparel, and special invitations to annual events. Members also receive a monthly newsletter. Die-hard fans have the option to become "VIPs" when they chip in $250, which gives them access to training camp, private autograph sessions, and limited-edition merchandise. Imagine the buzz the Ravens could create if they let women play the game!

Create a group. Make people feel that they are a part of something special. Then sit back and watch them talk about it while they wear their logo apparel and act as walking billboards for your business. It is a sight to behold.

Stunts

The Oscar Meyer Weiner Mobile. The Goodyear Blimp. Nathan's Famous Hot Dog Eating contest. They are all terrific examples of how to get people talking about a company. Follow their examples, and do something fun, out of the ordinary, or just plain silly. Watch people sit up and take notice of your company's name. Once they have heard your name, they are more likely to check you out — even if you are not into scarfing down 40 hot dogs in two minutes.

For instance, a PR firm in Edison, New Jersey landed clients simply based on the way the staff dressed. While the rest of the country was indulging in Casual Friday, the Pollack Agency went in the opposite direction and instituted Formal Friday. The firm's directors felt that the staff takes their jobs more seriously when they are in business attire so they took it one step further, and now the employees work decked out in ball gowns and penguin suits. They report that they landed several clients who heard about the policy and felt it showed the firm's ability to do things differently. Plus, the employees got to wear those duds that usually just collect dust.

CASE STUDY: ROBERT BASSO

Advantage Payroll Services

114 New South Road

Hicksville, NY 11801

www.liadvantage.com

info@liadvantage.com

800-440-9003 - phone

516-931-8500 - fax

Robert Basso - President and Founder

Event marketing and participation in charitable events is not new for my business; I have hosted special events in the past, some large and some small. I always like to do things that people will remember. Once, we "launched" some new services with a special event at a restaurant at an airport, using the airport theme throughout the program. We gave the attendees a small balsa wood airplane with our logo on it, and everyone built their own plane. We went outside and launched them toward a target with the closest to the mark winning a prize — a personal airplane tour of Long Island. People still talk about this event and it was five years ago.

I am often involved with charities but I got involved in the Long Island Fight for Charity because I thought it would be an interesting, once-in-a-lifetime experience. This was being really involved; I was often in the ring with guys who were 40 to 60 pounds heavier than me. I took a lot of punches for this effort but it was worth it. People still ask me about my participation in that and other events, and these efforts have led directly to business referrals from people I don't even know.

Participating in the fight worked so well for me that I encouraged my top salesperson to do it, and he has participated in it for the past three years. If I could do it differently, I would have started letting people know about my involvement in the Fight for Charity much sooner to build bigger buzz. I also would have hosted my own event to go along with the boxing match to help raise more money. It is hard to judge if the boxing event actually led to

CASE STUDY: ROBERT BASSO

getting a specific piece of business; however, the word-of-mouth attention we received from this event definitely translated into business.

I always try different approaches for promoting my business; I have to because we are a small company with a limited budget. By being different and involved in many activities like this, we can create marketing that has significant value. Other small businesses fail to do this and often wonder why they do not grow. When we generate buzz we also generate sales. After a thoughtful campaign, event, or series of activities, our sales team becomes very busy.

Half.com is another great example. The Web site launched during the dot-com boom and wanted to set itself apart, so it convinced tiny little Halfway, Oregon, a town with a population of 345, to change its name to Half.com for one year. For $100,000 and a new computer lab, the town agreed, and suddenly the suburb and the site were both enjoying coverage on *The Today Show* and in *The Wall Street Journal*.

Hollywood thrives on buzz marketing (along with plastic surgery and three-martini lunches) so it is no surprise when movies use publicity stunts to help box office sales, and the more extreme, the better. The Batman movie *The Dark Knight* is just one example. In advance of the release, evangelists across the country were told to report to a nearby bakery, give them the name, "Robin Banks" (clever, huh?), and wait to receive a cake. Written in icing were the words, "Call me now!" with a phone number. When the recipients cut the cake, they find not a plain layer of devil's food but a bag marked "Evidence, Gotham City Police Department." Inside the bag is a cell phone, a Joker playing card, and a note:

Wow. You really took the cake! Now put the icing on it. Call immediately from this phone and this phone only.

Do not give the phone number to anyone else. Let's hope your fellow goons come through as well as you. Once all the layers are in place, you'll all get your just desserts. I'm a man of my word.

After calling the number, recipients got a message on their new phone reading, "Good work, clown! Keep this phone charged and with you at all times. Don't call me. I will call you…eventually."

What a fantastic marketing campaign. Certainly, anyone who received a cake would tell anyone and everyone they knew about the adventure, all the while relaying that it was in conjunction with the upcoming release of the new Batman movie. Holy Batmobile, Robin! We have a publicity stunt on our hands!

Freebies

Most everyone loves to get something for free. Even if it is something they do not want, do not need, or do not ever use, they get that feeling of a kid trick-or-treating and that can translate into customer loyalty — or at least customer advertising.

Take the giveaways at trade shows. You may not need another coffee mug or a cool new lanyard, but you know your kids may like it, or you could use a spare at the office. So, you pick it up and maybe use it once or twice. You get that "I got something free" buzz, and others see the logo of the vendor. Also, if the vendor made any kind of impression on you at all, you may share that with someone, who may research that vendor the next time he or she is looking for a quote. Either way, you probably made your kid happy or at least have an extra mug on your desk to hold pencils.

Most trade show giveaways will not rival Dunlop's offer of free tires. The manufacturer gave away a free set of tires to people who would let them tattoo their logo on their bodies. It may sound a bit extreme (just a tad, eh?) but plenty of people took the company up on it. Fifty people took the plunge immediately and hundreds more signed up on a waiting list to get inked. Provide incentives for people and watch them fling some word of mouth around better than any off-roader could.

There is no need to wait for the next tradeshow to give away free merchandise and spark a buzz campaign. Freebies can be given anywhere at any time. Witness the Chipotle example. When he opened the Denver-based restaurant in 1993, owner Steve Ells had only $85,000 to cover every expense. There was simply no room in the budget for any kind of advertising. So Ells did what any smart businessman would do — he gave away his product. Literally, he just started handing out free burritos. When the Timothy J. McVeigh trial was held in Denver in 1997, he regularly delivered free food to the hordes of reporters camped out at the courthouse. It really helped spread the word about the restaurant's tasty twist on Mexican food.

Now, well more than a decade later, Chipotle still gives food away. When it opened a new store in Manhattan in 2006, it gave away burritos to 6,000 people — 6,000! Cost of the free food? Roughly $35,000, probably the same amount that a half-page ad would have cost. Instead of an ad that would have gone straight into most people's recycling bins, the company claimed 6,000 new spokespeople who were happy to tell others how good its food tasted.

Adidas used "Fevercards" in 2002 to spread brand advocacy among customers. Web site visitors could order free personalized contact cards featuring Adidas brand artwork on one side and the visitor's contact information on the other side. The company printed and mailed one million cards within 46 days to fans in 180 countries. Follow-up marketing shows 78 percent of the cards were handed out and 65 percent of the time it resulted in a conversation about the brand.

Depending on your business, consider writing an email newsletter. "Without a doubt, the most powerful thing you can give away is a free weekly email newsletter," advises Andy Sernovitz in his book *Word-of-Mouth Marketing*. "It is easy to produce, relevant to the reader, and easy to pass along. If you do not have an email newsletter, start one today." I think it depends on your business, but Andy is a big believer that people want to hear what you have to say. Moreover, if just one person forwards your free email instead of deleting it, you have just spread the buzz a little broader.

Along with freebies come "two-fers," otherwise known as two-for-one deals. Talk about a great way to multiply your word of mouth! If you give customers an extra of something, they are going to share it (or if they really like your product, they will keep the extra for themselves, which means they are probably already spreading some good WOM about you). When they share, they talk. Consider the free subscriptions *Reader's Digest* has been offering for a couple of years. My in-laws have subscribed to the magazine for years and, suddenly, the publisher gave them an offer to share a free subscription. They chose us, and now we are also regular readers thanks to the free introduction.

Two-fers work well for many types of businesses. Offers for ice cream stores, gym memberships (see how I put those two together in the same example?), and even oil changes will help one customer spread some word of mouth about a company to a friend or family member. Sure, you absorb the cost of one giveaway, but once that new prospect gets a taste of your terrific product and your unrivaled customer service, they will be hooked too.

Limited Supply

Nothing sparks interest as quickly as knowing that people may not be able to get their hands on something they want. Whether it is the price of oil driving up the price of gasoline and sparking a nationwide fear of a gas shortage, or nerve-wrecked parents trying to find a Cabbage Patch Kid doll during the holidays in the early 1980s, there is something about knowing you got an item that someone else wanted that makes you feel special. Like the eBay tagline, "Shop Victoriously" implies, people like to win. Try instituting something of your business or service that is available for a limited time only and see how well it works.

With no money spent on marketing, Google launched Gmail and made the accounts available to only a few people who were considered "Power Users." The name alone imbues prestige! Other people who wanted Gmail accounts bid for them on eBay. Imagine! Something that was free for some got others interested enough to pay for it. It was seen as something prestigious because so few were created.

Or try the Marines way — the few, the proud, the hard to find. That is what Paddi Lund did. Inside the book *Building the Happiness-Centred Business*, the publisher included an option to receive an email with pertinent information about the author and where to find the book (which is not widely available). The instructions actually walk the reader through forwarding an email about the book to help spread the word, saying, "In the best way you know how, tell the story of Paddi and his book, how you heard of it, and why you liked it so much. Then forward this message to those whom you really feel will enjoy Paddi's unique approach of happiness through simple systems in business." By making it a little more difficult to get the book and a lot more mysterious to share it, the publisher manages to make it seem like a special secret that readers can share with friends. Brilliant!

Tracking Devices

A critical part of word-of-mouth marketing is tracking how well your campaign is faring. After all, you are already listening to the feedback, right? Tracking it just means taking it a step further and measuring exactly how much buzz is being generated and how effective it is. Good news for small business owners: There are plenty of good tracking devices out there that will not cost you a cent.

After-Word

- Craft a message that is easy to understand and convey. You will not generate good word of mouth if your message gets garbled along the way; you will only generate confusion (and there is enough of that in the world already, believe me).

- Seek out those who are already speaking well of you. These are the people who respond positively to surveys, fill out glowing comment cards, or blog about how great your product is. They are a vital component to a successful word-of-mouth campaign.

- Listen to what people are saying about you, especially if it is negative. It gives you a chance to turn potential bad publicity into good buzz.

- Utilize publicity stunts, fan clubs, and free giveaways to get people to notice your company.

- Create a demand for your product by offering it in (carefully) limited quantities (too little is not enough to feed a buzz campaign, too much defeats the purpose).

A Word From the Experts

Michael Guld is an expert business development specialist and creator of the public radio show, "Talking Business with Michael Guld."

"Referrals are key to spreading word of mouth, so why not give people a reason to send people your way? Think about the biggest incentive you can offer. It could be a free oil change or gas card if you're in automotive service. Banks can offer cash back. An eldercare facility might offer to save money off next month's rent. Find the right trigger point for your audience and the right amount to offer. If you don't offer enough incentive for someone to raise an eyebrow, you haven't done yourself any good."

— Expert Michael Guld

For-Words

Rumors. Gossip. Innuendo. Since the beginning of time, people have been itching to share something juicy with others. It appeals to that whole human connection thing: "I know something that you don't and I cannot wait to share it with you."

When it comes to marketing, that undeniable desire to share is a goldmine. It is every marketer's dream to have the public spreading a brand's message far and wide. Fortunately, when the World Wide Web came along, it facilitated a whole new phenomenon in marketing: viral messaging. From emails to games and music to videos, people just cannot get enough of sharing something they like with others.

Now if only I could convince my kids of the benefits of sharing…

This chapter covers:

- An introduction to viral marketing

- Viral videos

- The elements of a successful viral campaign

VIRAL MARKETING

While it sounds about as appealing as morning sickness, viral marketing is an inexpensive and incredibly effective way to market a business worldwide in an unbelievably quick fashion. Unlike morning sickness, you may actually enjoy getting it. It is based on sending something online that is then forwarded — by intent, not by a computer virus. (Hence, the chapter title: forwards…forwords. Geez, at least I think it is clever.)

Like other forms of word-of-mouth marketing, viral messages enjoy a greater impact because they are forwarded from friend to friend. That is also what makes them so cost effective — you do not spend money to distribute your message to individual consumers.

Also like WOMM, viral marketing is becoming more and more popular. A Jupiter Communications survey shows that 80 percent (yes, that is 80) of online companies do some sort of viral messaging. And they are getting amazing visibility as a result; 81 percent of people pass along viral messages to at least one person. Nearly half of all people will forward a viral message to two or three people. There is a lot of world to cover; the statistics show viral marketing makes it pretty darn easy to span the globe.

Hotmail got its start with a viral marketing campaign in 1996. Hotmail users were converted into brand advocates by attaching a small message that read, "To get your FREE email account go to Hotmail.com" to every email they sent. Recipients would see the message and join the Hotmail ranks. It was an unparalleled success: The email service spent only $500,000 on marketing to land 12 million subscribers in a year and a half.

But viral marketing does not have to be sent as an email. It can take the form of advergames, images, video clips, or text messages. YouTube, Facebook, and MySpace are all seen as examples of viral marketing. Videos are posted for all to see and anyone can forward a particularly well-liked clip to his or her own social network.

Viral Videos

Gregg and Evan Spiridellis, owners of **JibJab.com**, created a funny parody of the 2004 presidential campaign called "This Land." The animated cartoon lampoons President Bush and John Kerry and sped across the Internet like a cat chasing its tail. The brothers released it to the 130,000 people who subscribed to their email newsletters and within days, millions of requests poured in. Painting equally unflattering pictures of both presidential candidates, the piece appealed to left- and right-wingers alike. A political historian in Nevada even asked for a copy of it, saying that 100 years from now, it would help define the 2004 election. The brothers were overnight sensations, making the rounds on morning newscasts and late-night talk shows, all the while touting their small little start-up company to the world. The move cost them little more than time, and it gained them a worldwide audience.

If a viral video is in your future to help spread buzz about your business, consider the following characteristics that most successful viral videos share. They are:

- Short
- Authentic
- Visually appealing
- Original

CASE STUDY: GREGG SPIRIDELLIS

JibJab Media, Inc.

209 Main Street, Suite 4

Venice, CA 90291

www.jibjab.com

310-314-4375

Gregg Spiridellis - Cofounder

We started our company in 1999 during the first dot-com boom. We knew that presidential elections were big cultural media events because we had created a viral video for the 2000 election. During that cycle, we had about 5 million page views and we knew from that experience that presidential elections were well suited to viral entertainment videos.

From that first experience, we knew that we needed to build our core audience. For four and a half years we were diligent about building our email list, so when we created "This Land" in 2004 we had about 130,9000 people on our email list. All we did was send the video to them with no money spent on advertising.

We normally average about 40,000 video streams a day. The first day out of the box, "This Land" did 150,000 video streams, and by day three, it was 500,000 a day. We were featured on *The Tonight Show*, *The Today Show*, and ABC News named us "People of the Year." You can't buy that kind of media exposure. It was our stated objective to become a national brand but after doing it for almost five years, we didn't have a real sense as to how fast it could become that big.

Viral video can be a great tool. There might be more effective tools out there for other businesses; viral might not be right for every message. The main thing is to look at who you are trying to reach and what you are trying to say, and whether viral is the right way to reach them. Really focus on your core audience and what you want to accomplish. It is hard to beat online word of mouth because it is just so easy once you have your core audience targeted.

KEY ELEMENTS

Like "This Land," they are one-of-a-kind experiences that draw viewers in and make them excited to share with other people. Some viral marketing strategies work; some do not. But there are some basic elements to include that may put your viral efforts in the "Most Likely to Succeed" category. The first is pretty simple: People like free stuff. Promise a freebie, like newsletters, games, samples, or a free download that carries your marketing message, and watch people go wild for your viral. Take the music group Radiohead, who took a spin on the viral marketing go-round when it announced in 2007 that it would give away its music free. Fans simply needed to go to the Radiohead Web site and download the latest album. In return, the group asked fans to donate however much money they felt appropriate. The band sold 1.2 million album downloads the first day and the average fan had donated $8 for a total gross of more than $9 million. Not bad for one day's sales on a marketing budget of next to nothing.

Another vital element to successful viral marketing: it is relatable. People are drawn to messages that ring true to them or things that feel familiar. Just like comfort food, it is satisfying to read or hear something that reminds people of something they already know, and it is a powerful way to get people to relate to your product or brand.

QAS, an Experian company that handles address verification, struck a familiar chord in its viral game that is reminiscent of the video game Pac-Man. The company wanted to create a game that would educate customers and prospects about its business, so it hired a Web design firm to design a Flash-based game. Called "The Great Delivery Race," the game lets players move items from one location to another across suburban streets while overcoming obstacles in their path. While at first blush it may not remind you of the company's focus of address verification, it is meant to remind players of the importance of delivering items to the right address. Anyone who has ever dealt with lost packages (which probably encompasses anyone who has ever shipped a holiday gift) can relate.

CareerBuilder.com created the Age-o-Matic campaign, a viral marketing effort that enables people to see the horrific effects of job dissatisfaction. The program let viewers upload a photo of themselves, answer questions about how much their job stinks, and then automatically age-progressed the photo to demonstrate how they would look if they stayed in their soul-sucking job. CareerBuilder took it one step farther, enabling the geriatric image to say anything viewers typed in and letting them email the whole frighteningly funny package to anyone.

CareerBuilder.com did no advertising, no promotion. The company simply featured the tool on a few CareerBuilder sites. Without a single dollar spent on advertising, the Age-o-Matic campaign took on a life of its own, garnering nearly 50 million media impressions in one month. Roughly two million unique visitors personally witnessed how they would look in the year 2057 — or how their appearance would be altered by a heinous job. It was personal, relatable, and funny, and it sparked great word of mouth at no cost to the company.

A key component to a viral piece is that it makes people feel something — anything. Humor works but so do sympathy and anger. If you get people riled up about your viral marketing efforts, they are a lot more likely to spread the message.

For example, most people have at one time or another cursed the printer they were working with for being inept. Naturally it is understood that whatever snafu occurred was due to the printer's fault and not operator error. Be that as it may, Samsung played on that frustration recently when it used viral gaming to increase brand awareness. The corporation wanted more people to know it has a line of commercial laser printers; specifically it wanted to target IT professionals who were unaware that the company even made printers. (Samsung is more widely known for being a consumer electronics purveyor as opposed to business products.) To poke fun at the industry's frustration with a lack of reliable printers, the corporation created the "Destroy a Printer" game. Players get weapons, including a baseball bat, with which to beat the crap out of a printer in a dark back alley. At the same time, the printer taunts the player with phrases like "My grandma hits harder" and "Oh. You're still here?" The pass-along rate was not as high as Samsung might have hoped but the game caught the attention of bloggers everywhere and resulted in an average of 15,000 unique visitors to the company's Web site.

Dove created the "evolution" viral video, which featured a female model sans makeup undergoing a beauty transformation. In a clip that is just over a minute long, myriad makeup artists and stylists transformed the woman into a breathtakingly exquisite billboard model. Once the makeup and hair was complete, viewers watched every change as her image was then enhanced via technology to make her neck look longer, her eyes look bigger and her overall appearance more alluring. The final shot showed the finished model on a billboard and ended with the phrase, "No wonder our perception of beauty is distorted." Dove's piece went far beyond any suggestion of selling soap — it was aimed at getting people to rethink their idea of what makes a person attractive. Tying in strategically to the company's Campaign for Real Beauty, Dove used the viral video to make people reconsider what beauty really is.

An outstanding example of making people feel something — in this case, frustration — is Burger King's marketing campaign called the "Whopper Freakout." If you missed it, it is well worth visiting **www.whopperfreakout.com** to see for yourself. In the video, Burger King captures customers' reactions when told that the Whopper, the main staple of the fast food royalty, as been discontinued because it was "too popular." The reactions are priceless! I dare anyone who likes a good gag not to be amused. You would think that the chain had just announced the end of the french fry or that apple pie was no longer American. To help give the viral piece more visibility, Burger King used some of the same footage for a 30-second TV commercial of the same ilk. The results were two-fold: one, the public at large enjoyed a good laugh at the upset customers' responses and two, the Home of the Whopper enjoyed increased sales as a result of the joke. It was an extremely clever way to use a negative situation simply to highlight the burger's popularity. It was what you might call a whopper of a viral video!

When creating a viral piece, it is important to give people a place for feedback. You have gotten their attention with viral messaging; now listen to what they have to say about it. You may love the comments you read or you may hate them, but you need to create an atmosphere where people can dish about your piece. After all, that is what gets people talking about you.

Suave and Sprint together created "In the Motherhood," a series of webisodes featuring mothers in a variety of daily situations, including a child throwing a fit on a plane and a little girl locking her mom in the bathroom for hours. The pieces are short, funny, fun — and realistic. Beyond that, the Web site (**www.inthemotherhood. com**) features a community board where moms can vent about the episodes and relate their own challenging experiences in the maternal world.

One of the most crucial elements to a successful viral venture is making it easy to share. After all, if viewers cannot send it to others, your word of mouth is pretty much dead in the water, right? Viewers want to be able to download the content easily and forward it to others. Keep it simple for them and choose the most usable formats available. If you are lucky, your viewers will be so entranced by your video that they will want to put it on their own Web sites, which helps you spread the buzz that much faster. Consider bandwidth when you are creating, so that you do not limit who can showcase your campaign.

Dr. Pepper kept all that in mind when introducing its new cherry chocolate-flavored diet soda with a viral campaign. Instead of using its advertising agency, Young & Rubicam, the soft drink maker hired a New York production company to create a viral music video. The piece mimics music videos, showcasing Tay Zonday, best known for the song "Chocolate Rain," and rapper Mistah Johnson. The pair was surrounded by dancing women with skimpy clothes and the final product looked for the entire world like a video you would see on MTV. According to Dr. Pepper, the video had 300,000 hits in its first 24 hours and more than one million views within less than a week. The company still planned to utilize traditional media to launch the product in 2008, replete with TV and print ads, but chose to use nontraditional means to "talk" to consumers and get the buzz started early.

Companies are realizing that beyond games and videos, people are basically narcissistic. They like things that amuse them but they like it even more if they can see themselves in it or be a part of it. Personalized viral marketing is becoming more popular as more designers create campaigns that let viewers put their own personal touches on the message. For example, visitors to **www.munkyourself.com** can record a message in a chipmunk voice and send it to friends, all the while promoting the movie *Alvin and the Chipmunks*. More than 300,000 fans of the 2005 flick *Wedding Crashers* created "trailer crasher videos," placing their faces over the characters in the movie trailer.

However, personalized viral marketing is not limited to the big screen. OfficeMax created "Elf yourself" in 2006, a chance for viewers to upload personal photos of themselves to create dancing elves. The campaign drew more than 110 million visitors in its first two years. As a result of the initial success, the company added scroogeyourself.com the following year to further take advantage of the viral craze and showcase its brand during the all-important holiday shopping season. This is an important point; once you get word of mouth going, keep it going by creating sequels. You have their attention; hold on to it for dear life. Launch another viral campaign that builds on the first, features bloopers or out-takes, or gives a behind-the-scenes look. Anything that keeps people talking keeps word of mouth spreading.

Even if it means going to the dogs or cats. Purina launched doggy-email and kitty-email at **www.petcentric.com**, enabling viewers to create an email masterpiece using talking canines and cats in famous works of art. The 11-month campaign got one million users to upload photos of the pets and spend an average of five minutes on the brand's Web site. Did it sell more pet food? Maybe not, but if it gets people talking about the brand, that is a crucial component of word-of-mouth marketing.

Incentives work wonders. You can encourage people to share the message by offering a coupon or a discount for every time they forward it. This is perfectly acceptable as long as it is above-board and each person involved is aware that incentives are being provided.

Skeptics say viral marketing is not particularly beneficial to most branding efforts, pointing out that frequently the ad itself becomes well known but rarely brings anything back to the brand or results in more sales. While that is still being determined, one thing is certain: Viral marketing is not going anywhere anytime soon — except to others' computers. More than half of marketers who have done extensive work with viral marketing say they planned to launch multiple viral efforts throughout 2007. Additionally, 57 percent of survey respondents said they were planning at least one viral campaign. Clearly, it is a growing mechanism to spread word of mouth. Your only question should be how to get in on the viral phenomenon as soon as possible.

Experienced viral marketers typically have several steps they follow to ensure as successful a campaign as possible.

Step One: Exploration. Who is most likely to forward your viral message? Which sites are most likely to be popular enough to help your viral piece spread? Knowing this ahead of time will help you ensure your viral message goes farther, faster.

Step Two: Incorporation. Mix your viral message in with other aspects of your marketing tactics. On its own, a viral piece is likely to suffer the fate the skeptics predict: either a fast death or one that does not bring anything to your brand. However, if you make viral marketing one part of your overall campaign, it is much more likely to be effective.

Step Three: Evaluation. As you would with most any kind of marketing campaign, create different viral models and test them based on creativity, messaging, and motivation. This phase enables you to predict with decent accuracy what to expect from your viral campaign.

Step Four: Interaction. Reach out to your customers and prospects with an email offer that they can use to forward to others to help generate more word of mouth. Remember, anything that can be forwarded is viral in nature, so make your campaign revolve around something that will get people jazzed up. It is a sure-fire way to ignite more exposure at less expense.

If used properly, viral marketing can be a highly effective tool in your word-of-mouth arsenal. It hearkens back to that old commercial by Faberge Organics shampoo. "You tell two friends, and they tell two friends, and so on, and so on, and so on." (But imagine it without the multiple images of the Stepford-like model on your widescreen TV.)

After-Word

- Viral marketing is a vital and effective way to stimulate word of mouth. Anything that catches people's attention and is easy to forward will help your company generate buzz.

- Videos are one of the best-known forms of viral marketing, but they are not the only kind. Consider creating games, images, or text messages showcasing your business and start getting them forwarded across the Web.

- Viral marketing is more successful when people can relate to what they are seeing. Making your viral piece relatable is a good way to get the public to relate to your product or brand.

- Make the recipient feel something when they receive your viral piece. Emotions are powerful tools. Whether they get angry or laugh out loud, triggering emotions will help people remember you.

- Give people a place for feedback, and listen to what they have to say about your viral campaign. Tweak it, if necessary, to make it even more effective.

- If you manage to create a successful campaign, do not let it fizzle out. Build on it. Create a sequel. Showcase bloopers or out-takes. Give people a behind-the-scenes look at what it took to create your masterpiece.

- Offer up freebies or discounts for people who forward your viral marketing. Perhaps they can print out a coupon after hitting "send" or fill out a form for free merchandise. Free is a powerful incentive.

Is That Even a Word?

MANY people keep diaries or journals to record their thoughts and feelings. When I was little, I kept a diary under strict lock and key — until I lost the key. My thoughts were private, only meant for me. (And they stayed that way — I never did find the sucker.)

So what is different? Why is everyone in the world putting their every thought and feeling out for the general public to read and debate?

What changed is the way people communicate with each other. As our society finds more ways to connect — cell phones, Blackberries, emails, and so forth — weblogs are just one more vehicle for conversations. When used as a marketing tool, they are a priceless way to spread word of mouth. And you do not have to worry about losing the key. (Just do not forget your password.)

This chapter covers:

- An introduction to blogs

- Step-by-step blog creation

- Choosing a topic

- Promoting a blog

- Blog advertising

BLOG MARKETING

As unattractive as the word feels in your mouth, weblogs, or blogs, as they are known, can be immensely effective marketing tools. They are frequently updated online diaries or journals containing opinions, information, and links. And they are basically free marketing, or nearly so.

While at first blush they appear to be one-sided musings, blogs can help establish expertise, spark sales, and even open a dialogue with consumers. According to an August 2007 Nielson survey, 61 percent of people trusted "consumer opinions posted online," otherwise known as blogs. Contrast that to the 56 percent of people who trusted TV ads and the 54 percent who put their trust in radio commercials and you will see the impact that blogs can have in a word-of-mouth campaign.

While they all share the name "blog," there are many different types of blogs that can be used in word-of-mouth marketing: blogvertorials, corporate blogs, and faux blogs.

Words are constantly evolving and as new as blogs are, the word itself has already morphed. First, there were advertorials, editorial posts that sought to flaunt a product or service while making a point. Now there are "blogvertorials," venues that encourage third-party posts or reviews and may help foster communication between a company and its customers. Think of them as open houses to which the press might be invited — they are a place to help plant the seeds of a new word-of-mouth marketing campaign, offer samples or other freebies, and get consumer reactions to products.

Stonyfield Farm, an organic U.S. dairy, uses its "Cow munity" blog to communicate with customers and employees. It offers fun and interactive pages to promote industry news, new products, campaigns for eating healthier and better nutrition with recipes, "moosletters," and contests. The site even enables visitors to blog with a farmer via "The Bovine Bugle." It is a moo-ving example of blogging at its best.

Corporate blogs promote a company. Often penned by high-profile or high-ranking executives, they are designed to help consumers feel more connected to a brand. It can be used to announce new products or services or react to public criticism or other issues. It is seen as slightly less formal than a traditional press release although the two accomplish similar goals.

Microsoft has a blog called Scobleizer, written by Robert Scoble, one of the company's technical gurus. It is written in a very warm, personal tone to attract readers and help them envision the software titan as more gentle than giant.

Delta.com general manager Laura Hunnicut pens "Under the Wing," the airline's attempt to land more satisfied customers. It introduces pilots, planes, destinations, and mileage programs and enables fliers to leave feedback about their experiences with Delta. One poster wanted to know how to get over her fear of flying. The site establishes the airline as an expert source of information regarding those giant aluminum birds in the sky.

Faux blogs are a big no-no when it comes to word-of-mouth marketing. Also known as "flogs," they are one of the fastest ways to stop good buzz in its tracks and stir up a fresh pot of revolt. They are written to appear as though they are penned by the enthusiastic members of the general public but are, in fact, written by company agents or employees to generate some buzz. The problem is once it is known that the blog is a fake, people often turn their back on the product or the company being hyped.

Wal-Mart launched the flog "Wal-Marting Across America," ostensibly written by two people who could not get enough of the giant yellow smiley face bouncing around and chopping prices. They decided to journey across the country in an R.V. and blog about their experiences at Wal-Mart stores along the way. In truth, two people did make the trip for the blog but after the news leaked that Wal-Mart had funded their travels, the smiley face was not smiling quite as broadly.

Also see Chapter 10 to read about Dr. Pepper's flog, which resulted in a flop of a product.

But blogs can be enormously successful — when utilized properly — and can reach millions of people in a nanosecond. When D.C.-based lawyer Megan Cosby started her blog, **PoliChicksOnline. com**, she was just looking for a way to share her interest in politics. She did not have her eye on a post at the White House; she simply felt that all too often politics is presented in an academic and boring way. So she started sharing her views online. She launched the site in August 2007 and told about 20 friends about her venture. Within less than two months, she was averaging more than 3,300 hits per day. Those 20 people shared her URL with others they knew, and polichicksonline.com was an almost-overnight destination for those who wanted to talk about politics without being bored to tears.

CREATING A BLOG

So you are sold on the idea of blogs but you do not know where to start? You are in the right place — again.

There are several ways to launch your own blog. Many Internet sites offer free blog hosting, or you can research Web hosts to do something more unique. If you already have a Web site, you might consider using something like WordPress or Blogspot. Both are free personal publishing platforms that will help you match the look and feel of your existing site. Choose a domain name that helps further your brand and that complements your site. Once you have installed the necessary WordPress plug-ins or add-ons, you are ready to write your first post.

Before you put pen to paper or digit to keyboard, first do some research. Check out the competition. Who else in your industry has a blog and what are they saying? You do not want to duplicate something that is already out there. Once you are ready to write, keep a few things in mind:

- **Pick a topic and stick to it.** It is easy to start writing and to get off topic but you will need to stay focused to keep your reader's attention. Having trouble coming up with a topic? Keep reading— help is on the way.

- **Keep your entry as short as possible.** People read blogs to get quick information and opinions. They are not expecting (nor do they want) the virtual edition of *War and Peace*.

- **Create a schedule that is realistic.** Do not promise that you are going to blog three times a day and then find you only have time to post once a week.

Posting often will help train your readers to check out your blog regularly. Yes, you can actually train your readers! The downside? You need to keep it up. Readers will get turned off if they repeatedly find outdated information and they will find another blog to read.

Blogs are the facts and just the facts, with some opinion sprinkled in. Do not use your blog solely as a way to get back at someone. Use it as you would an editorial in the newspaper, to lay out your case and back it up with the truth.

Spell check, spell check, spell check. Once you have done that, proofread, proofread, proofread. After all, spell checking will only catch words that are spelled wrong but that will not ensure that your copy is perfect. Remember there is only one letter difference between "public" and "pubic" but that one letter could make a huge difference in how your message is perceived.

Lastly, look at a blog as a long-term investment. Do not write one or two blog entries, decide they did not generate enough traffic and give up. It takes time for people to find you, to read your post, and decide it is worth their while to come back for more. Stick it out for a while and see what is working. If you find you are not getting the responses you hoped for, evaluate your blog with a critical eye. You may be able to turn it around totally just by making a few small changes as outlined above.

What Should You Blog About?

Good blogs have several things in common: There is no question who is writing them or affiliated with them, they are authentic and unique, they are written with passion (who wants to read something by someone who is bored with the topic?), and they encourage readers to think about, respond to, or discuss the topic.

Nevertheless, you cannot write with passion unless you are passionate about the subject. Consider what makes you tick — or what ticks you off. Identify your interests and jot them down as potential blog topics. There is an old saying, "Write what you know." This is the perfect place to follow that advice. Besides, if you try to blog about something you are not passionate about, you are not likely to stick with it. It will become as tedious as that final set of reps you swore you would finish when you started exercising.

Blogs can be fun. In fact, they should be fun. Ice cream flavor developer Denali Flavors figured that out when it created Moosetopia, the blog written by the company moose-cot, I mean, mascot. Yes, it is a blog penned by a moose who details his traveling adventures. Denali created the ever-popular flavor of ice cream called Moosetracks and wanted to get more visibility and increase sales. The company was not content with just one blog, though; it created three. In addition to Moosetopia, there is the Denali Flavors blog, which provides behind-the-licks information, new product ideas, and small business issues. Finally, the company offers Team Moose Tracks, a blog focused on the company's cycling team that raises money for charitable organizations.

A critical component of the blogs' successes are the customer emails. Get a load of this one:

> After exhaustive study and deep soul searching, I have come to the conclusion that the primary reason Saddam was such a dangerous bully is simply because he didn't have access to Denali ice cream. Luckily for America, your wonderful product is available to the vast majority of patriotic citizens, providing us our Daily Dose of Denali. As a good corporate citizen, you have the power

to ensure world peace and eliminate strife among nations. Get your wonderful ice cream products quickly to all the trouble spots of the world!

If three blogs hosted by the same business sounds like overkill, it has not proven to be the case with Denali. The company boasts an increase of 18 percent more Web site visits and 10 percent more hits. What is more, visitors spend 26 percent more time on the site (which must mean a lot of melted ice cream) and revenue increased more than eight percent. Attracting more customers and keeping them longer can go a long way toward spreading buzz — and brain freeze.

The folks at Quicken Loans wanted to start a corporate blog but they did not know what to write about. They considered the obvious: mortgages, finance, credit, and real estate. They discounted every one of them because they felt that the topics might bore readers to tears and then they remembered what they consider special at Quicken Loans: their people and their stories. They created the DIFF blog (they like to say that is what makes them DIFF, do not ask why) and got plenty of positive attention. Feedback came from all over, including kudos for talking about something other than their business on a corporate blog.

Picking a popular topic is also important. People have to want to read what you are blogging about. Evidently, with a global audience chances are that someone somewhere shares your passion on a topic, whether it is politics or Pollyanna. Remember that what is popular today may not be next month, so do your best to keep your finger on the pulse of the public. Trends make great blog topics as long as you catch them on the way in instead of the way out.

CASE STUDY: ANDY ABRAMSON

Comunicano

1155 Camino Del Mar

Suite 512

Del Mar, CA 92014

www.comunicano.com

858-523-1800 - phone

Andy Abramson - Blogger

I started to blog in 2004 when I realized there was a big gap between the outreach efforts to bloggers and how news was being reported in Voice over Internet Protocol (VoIP). When I started, the blog had four goals: 1) to talk to traditional media and help them understand VoIP as a subject matter expert, 2) to provide clarity so I could speak and moderate at conferences, 3) to make new friends, and 4) to attract new business. I felt that if I attracted the right type of attention, a large group of companies would come to us and sure enough, that happened.

A former board member of a client of mine came and asked for my help to launch a VoIP company. One thing led to another; I got one client, and another, and another, then Nokia came and asked, "How would you approach blogger relations, because Nokia has tried twice." All of a sudden this one-person shop became Nokia's blogger relations overnight.

Fast-forward to 2008 and I now have 15 people working for me, with a client base from Israel to Australia, and a growing reputation for being the right group to talk to if you want to do blogger relations correctly.

Every company we advise and provide services to has some component of blogger relations in the communications mix. My position is respected as an authority in the blogging world because I also blog. It has brought a lot of new business to us, as well as third parties who rely on us for our opinions including reporters, Wall Street analysts, and venture capitalists.

CASE STUDY: ANDY ABRAMSON

Where people fail with blogs is that they lack transparency. If I am writing about a client in my blog, I reference them as a client. There is a lot of corporate blogging going on with companies coming in and blogging for their clients, but making it appear as it is the company, not the agency. We're not into generating false stories that are planted. That is where credibility comes in. The most important things in successful blogging are clarity, transparency, honesty, credibility, and having fun.

The day I put my blog up was the day I knew I'd generated something truly buzz worthy. Within six months I had clients seeking me out. The blog has been the single and only marketing vehicle I have used, and everyone who has come to us has been recommended or found us through the blogs, either mine, the agency's, or the blogs of bloggers who are our best reference.

PROMOTING YOUR BLOG

Three letters are imperative to expanding your blog's reach: RSS. It stands for Rich Site Summary and it is one of the best ways to let people know when you have updated content and info on your blog.

Other ways to get your blog noticed?

- Join a blog carnival (where every blogger who joins blogs about a topic, and each blog gets promoted).

- Participate in forums and other blogs. It is a great way to connect with individuals and demonstrate your expertise, all the while giving you a place to link back to your blog.

- Join Blogbust, the blog network that syndicates content at newspapers' Web sites including *USA Today* and Reuters.

- Submit to blog directories, Google sitemaps, and article directories.

- Buddy up with other bloggers. It is a great way to get more visibility and more credibility.

- Be a guest blogger. Offer a free blog posting to someone in your niche and let an entirely new audience get to know you.

- Join virtual groups like Yahoo! Groups, a whole network of people interested in the same thing you are and a built-in audience for your blog.

- Leave comments on other blogs. If you post a comment responding to what the initial entry is saying, you can then mention something relevant about your blog and post a link. Just resist the urge to go to every blog you read and say, "Hey! Check out my blog!" with a link. That is considered spamming and most impolite.

- Make your subscription options obvious, offer an email alternative to RSS, and ask for the subscription.

- Offer a freebie, like a free report, white paper, eBook available in PDF, or e-course. This will likely work the best when you tie email subscriptions in as a way to entice readership.

- Create a dedicated subscription landing page whose sole purpose is to get readers to subscribe. Use your blog, AdWords, or any other source to drive traffic to it.

BLOG **A**DVERTISING

If you are not quite ready to launch your own blog but you see the potential to reach customers, you might consider marketing yourself on someone else's blog. Blog ad campaigns can be a relatively inexpensive way to spread the word about your business.

Great places to start a blog advertising campaign include Blogads, AdBridge, Feedburner, and Weblogs, Inc.

Things to keep in mind before creating a blog ad:

- **Make it fun and different.** Blog readers are inundated with the same overwhelming number of messages as the rest of the world so make your ad stand out. Be humorous. Be edgy. Be noticeable! Or risk being overlooked along with that ad for herbal organ enhancements.

- **What have you done for them lately?** Readers do not care about what you do; they want to know what you do for them. There is a difference the size of Al Sharpton's hairstyle. Get to the point quickly and tell them exactly how your product or service will make their life better.

- **Go clean or be invisible.** At the risk of sounding patronizing, there are a plethora of words on a blog. When you design your ad, make it clean and easy to read. Use your white space wisely. Do not be tempted to clutter your ad with too many graphics or other flashy fodder, or it is likely to be overlooked.

- **Take advantage of the available elements.** Think of your ad as a text newsletter. Use a headline to capture attention.

Use HTML in the text to make important points stand out and catch the attention of skim readers. Keep it short, sweet, and easy to read.

- **In this case, change is good.** Actually, it is better than good; it is imperative. You may have bought a one-week slot for your ad to run, but then switch it up a bit. Try running a different message every few days so that you offer readers some variety. As a result, if one piece does not get readers to click through, you are not stuck with it for a week. Perhaps you will have more luck with the next one — but only if you change it up.

- **Remember, bloggers are influencers.** They speak (or write) their mind and let others respond to their opinions. They are highly connected to friends, family, and colleagues through technology. That said, they may also be more prone to be cynical and skeptical so forget trying to catch their attention with anything other than honest and creative advertising.

- **Target your audience.** The same ad will not work effectively on different blogs. For instance, if you are targeting mothers who stay at home with their children, craft an ad with them in mind. Create a totally different ad for a blog that is aimed at college students, and yet another one at mixologists. Each group has its own blog for a reason; each requires a unique approach.

- **Inform your audience.** Deliver your message but do not sell to the readers. Remember, these are influencers who can spot advertising a World Wide Web away, and will not hesitate to call you on it in a public way.

AFTER-WORD

- Blogs can be an immensely effective marketing tool. After all, blogs are read and linked to by people all over the world. What better way to get your company on the map?

- Giving bloggers a chance to review a new product before it launches can help generate powerful word of mouth.

- Corporate blogs may help consumers and employees feel more connected to a company, promoting brand loyalty and a sense of being "in the know."

- Faux blogs, or flogs, are a breach of ethics and a potential marketing nightmare. Trying to pretend that you are a third party writing glowing recommendations about your product is likely to backfire in a big way. Do not go there.

- Many Internet sites offer free blog hosting, so it is a no-cost way to get people talking about your business.

- Choose a topic and stay focused. Be passionate about what you are writing. Always spell check and proofread before you post your musings to avoid potential embarrassment.

- Promote your blog with RSS feeds. Participate in others' blogs and link back to your own. Be a guest blogger on someone else's site. Join online groups to help network among others who share an interest in your product or services.

- Try blog advertising. Make your ad stand out, make it clean but attention-getting, and update your ad frequently to better your chances of getting noticed.

- Tell readers what you can do for them. Inform them but do not use your ad to sell. Target your audience with an ad that is specific to them, but change the ad for different target audiences.

In Words & Out Words

It is 6 p.m. and your family just sat down to dinner. The phone rings. It is Murphy's Law — it must be a telemarketer, right? If you lived in my house you would either a) choose not to answer the phone, b) pick it up and slam it down without saying a word, or c) tell them, "Thanks, but no thanks," and hang up. Telemarketing is outdated, desperate, disruptive, and rarely successful.

E-mail marketing, on the other hand, is skyrocketing. Businesses love it: it is an affordable and quick way to reach a vast audience (and no one gets hung up on). Consumers prefer it: opt-in options let them to get the information they want from the businesses they choose at a time when it is convenient for them to read it (and no one gets hung up on).

This chapter covers:

- An overview of e-mail marketing

- Tips to successful e-mail marketing

- E-mail newsletters

- Creating lists

- Legal concerns about e-mail marketing

E-MAIL MARKETING

E-mail in-boxes are a fantastic place to spread word of mouth. While that may sound sarcastic, take the message seriously. And before you turn your nose up at one of the oldest online communication tools in favor of trendier blogs and online discussion groups, take a look at this statistic: A Pew Internet and American Life Project survey found that 91 percent of Internet users between the ages of 18 and 64 send or read e-mail — far more than any social network. Think of the audience you can target!

In addition, when you communicate to a mailing list of subscribers, it can generate a discussion list which lets all recipients communicate directly. It is a way for businesses to educate customers and potential clients, as well as foster great communication between those who want to discuss a brand, product, or service.

Some people are quick to toss any marketing e-mail in the computer wastebasket so before you hit your internal "delete" button, hear me out. E-mail marketing can be very effective. Let us explore its advantages.

When you are communicating with your customers via e-mail, you are staying in touch, you are on their radar, and you are in their line of sight: all powerful parts of cultivating a customer sales force.

E-mail marketing keeps your business in your customers' minds even when it is not your peak season. Find a reason to e-mail at least monthly so you will be top of mind. It helps cultivate your current customers into repeat buyers.

E-mail campaigns can also be a boon for prospecting. Furthermore, when you are sending to a list of potential new consumers, you are able to reach a large group at a relatively low cost, which lowers the expense of trying to land new customers. Studies show it costs somewhere between five and seven times more money to market to new customers rather than existing ones. E-mail marketing is a major exception to that rule. Here is why:

- Compared to printed newsletters or direct mail, e-mail marketing is less expensive and more environmentally friendly. Think how many trees you can save!

- Nothing is faster than hitting the "send" button. You can update information daily, even instantly, for little or no cost, as opposed to waiting for a print run and a mail drop to happen.

- E-mail marketing lets you target your audience proactively to share your news and information. No more waiting for them to log on to your Web site.

- It is also easy to track. Whether you want to know how many people forwarded it, clicked through, or unsubscribed to the list, you can find the numbers you seek.

- You can also advertise on someone else's e-mail newsletter, sharing resources (like their mailing list) and cutting costs.

'TIS THE SEASON FOR E-MAILS

If you are a business owner with a seasonal business, e-mail marketing is a terrific way to generate sales during your off-season. For instance, most florists probably have more business than they can handle around Valentine's Day and Mother's Day. The rest of the year can be a totally different story. What if a florist used all of the other smaller holidays, like Teacher Appreciation Day, Grandparent's Day, or Administrative Assistants Day, to generate sales? Face it: we are a culture that has a holiday to mark just about everything — turn that into a selling point.

How? Say the florist e-mailed all of his customers a few weeks before the smaller holidays listed above. Say he also included a discount coupon in his e-mail, like a 15 percent savings on all orders. It might just be enough to get someone to think, "Geez, I really do think my kid's teacher is great. Maybe I should send her flowers." Or, for those who are not up to speed on Hallmark's special days, it can be easy to overlook something like Grandparent's Day. But if that florist sent you a reminder a few weeks ahead of time with an incentive discount, it could be enough to generate sales that otherwise would have been missed.

This same tactic can work wonders for other businesses that do seasonal work, like landscaping companies. Even during the winter, landscaping businesses can offer winterizing specials, deals on fall fertilizing, or pre-spring clean-up. Hardware stores could send e-mails with discounts on snowblowers, chemical salts, and rakes in the fall. Come midwinter, they could entice customers suffering from spring fever to stock up on mulch, pruning shears, or flower bulbs.

U.S. firms alone spent $400 million on e-mail marketing in 2006. And in 2007, 15 states were pushing for legislation that would block advertising mail, which would have an enormous impact on direct mail. Visibly, e-mail marketing has a lot going for it and is likely to have even more going for it in the future than advertising mail. That is not to say that e-mail marketing does not have its drawbacks.

As anyone with an e-mail account is well aware, too many companies engage in spam, sending unsolicited bulk e-mail. In fact, they have gotten so proficient at it that sometimes it is hard to tell the difference between a legitimate marketing message and spam. That means there is a chance your e-mail will be deleted before it is ever read, thus stopping that potential source of word of mouth from going any farther.

And thanks to spam, more filters are in place to help block unwanted e-mails. Although it is rare, those filters can occasionally also block legitimate commercial e-mails. Fortunately, opt-in advertising helps you get your message out without fear of being blocked. Opt-in e-mail marketing lets the consumer consent to receive your e-mails, ensuring they will not be blocked or deleted by any filters before they reach your target audience.

Opt-in is key to ensuring you keep your intended audience happy. To be sure, if you send unwanted e-mails with your company name, the reader automatically associates your name with junk — not exactly the first impression you want to create. Key point: Make any e-mail marketing program transparent. Let people know what they are signing up for. And for heaven's sake, if you tell them they can choose not to be part of it, honor that. No one likes to be duped. And if they are, the negative reaction can be devastating to your business.

MAKE IT COUNT

Making the most of your e-mail marketing means remembering

less is more. In other words, try not to overdo it. Here are a baker's dozen pointers:

1. Make your e-mail marketing campaign an opt-in experience, meaning you will only send commercial e-mails to recipients that have requested them by signing up for them at a Web site or on a special ad bane. Bulk e-mail marketing is not only annoying but typically it is unsuccessful. Not only that, but many Internet Service Providers (ISPs) will discontinue your account if they get complaints from people that you are sending unsolicited e-mails. That is not exactly the kind of word of mouth you are looking for, now is it?

2. Stick with easy-to-read and universal fonts supported by most computers. Be sure the text color stands out from the background; you need it to be easy to read to keep your audience engaged.

3. Minimize graphics — they often distract from your logo and your message, and they are not the point of your e-mail anyway.

4. Disable the images on your e-mail and see whether there is enough supporting text to capture someone's interest and entice them to read more.

5. Keep the overall size of the e-mail less than 50KB for consumer e-mails, or 75KB for businesses. Anything larger takes too long to load, costing you precious time with your audience.

6. Target your audience by including content that is relative to them. Do not send the same e-mail to existing customers

and potential customers; your message to each should be different.

7. Create a subject line that is short, catchy, and most of all, honest. Do not mislead people about the content of your e-mail — it is a big turnoff and a sure-fire way to be sure they will not read the next one you send.

8. Smart wording can make all the difference. Instead of writing, "Please send me your newsletter," try wording it, "Please notify me of sales and discounts." One is much more enticing than the other — and more likely to land you more sign-ups.

9. Keep the width of your HTML message under 650 pixels. Anything larger has the potential to get cut off in a preview panel which could give someone reason to delete.

10. Focus on one message. Cramming too much into one e-mail leaves the reader confused.

11. Include a visible, crystal-clear call to action. Do not leave readers wondering what they are supposed to do next.

12. Resend unopened e-mails. Three to four days after you do an e-mail blast, send a follow-up e-mail to those who chose not to open it the first time.

13. Even though your e-mail is set up as an opt-in, you should still include an unsubscribe line in case readers change their mind. Remember to also include a physical address and your privacy policy so recipients know who else may be getting their e-mail addresses.

E-MAIL NEWSLETTERS

In addition to sending out e-mail messages and incentives, a regular, well-written e-newsletter or e-zine can do wonders for engaging your audience. Think of it this way: e-mail campaigns are mainly effective at increasing sales; e-newsletters are a tool to educate and inform your audience over time. It is an effective technique to give advice and information about your product and your industry. It may not pay off with every issue, but the big payoff comes when a subscriber is ready to purchase — your business has the edge over the competition because you have been communicating with that prospect on a regular basis. You have kept their attention, built some credibility, and gained their trust. When you do that with a list of thousands of subscribers, it builds you a remarkable group of influentials to help spread the word of mouth about your company.

Your particular business or company will determine what your e-zine will be about. As long as you keep it centered on your readers' interests and how your brand can meet their needs, this is a powerful tool. However, do not fall into the trap of only using your newsletter to promote your work; it should be editorial in nature, including things like articles, case studies, statistics, product reviews, and how-to pieces. That does not mean you should shy away from all promotions — after all, you would not be sending it out if you did not have something to sell — but your main goal should be to interest, educate, and inform your readers.

To that end, try to keep your newsletter to a manageable length. If you can write it in one screen, with just a few graphics and headers, you stand a better chance of keeping your readers' interest. Use links to maximize the number of people who will click through to read articles, product reviews, and case studies instead of including all of the above in your initial e-mail. You are more likely to get the reader engaged that way.

Speaking of engaging the reader, make your e-zine or newsletter as interactive as possible. When you get them engaged, you greatly impact how loyal they are to your business and how much attention they pay to your venture. Get readers involved by including surveys. Not everyone will participate but some will, and it will give you a built-in piece for your next issue because you can share the results.

Another strong incentive to get readers to open your next issue? Invite them to ask questions of an expert. A real estate agent's newsletter might feature a mortgage banker one month, and readers could inquire about the best way to refinance, for instance. Or a beauty salon could invite readers to ask about the best ways to prolong hair color in color-treated hair, or how to make a manicure last. Make sure people know you will only be able to answer one or two questions per issue; that every question will be read but not all can be answered. Talk about a way to guarantee readers will stay tuned!

Strive to publish on a regular basis; weekly or biweekly is a good rule of thumb. It helps create continuity to publish more often; readers will not remember what they read a whole month ago. Whichever schedule you choose should fit both your budget and your time constraints so that you can maintain it on a long-term basis. Being consistent is the key: It does you no good to publish weekly for a while and then fall to every two weeks. In fact, that may do more harm than good, creating the impression that you are not a reliable provider. Readers of a well-written newsletter will look forward to receiving the next issue and you do not want to let them down.

Your e-mail newsletter can be published in text-only, HTML, or PDF. As long as it contains good information that is easy to read, the format does not matter too terribly much. Certainly, most readers will appreciate nice visual images but the quality of what you write is far more important than flashy graphics or headlines with a catchy font.

As with anything else related to word of mouth, you need to track your e-newsletter to determine its effectiveness. Most third-party e-mail management and delivery providers will track your publication based on the delivery rate (how many were received versus bounced back), the open rate (how many people took the time to read it), the click-through rate (showing you which links were popular and which were ignored), and the subscription rate (based on new subscribers and unsubscribes).

If you are willing to open your wallet, consider advertising in others' e-mail newsletters to generate more brand awareness and drive more traffic to your Web site. If you target another business whose audience is similar to yours, but not identical, you generate more prospects. It exposes you to people likely to support your business who are not already your customers. However, be certain you are targeting the right audience or it will not be a good fit.

GENERATING LISTS

Crafting the perfect e-mail sales message and e-zine is only half of the battle. When sent to the right people, an effective, targeted e-mail marketing campaign can turn leads into sales, drive traffic to your Web site, and get your word of mouth buzzing. No matter how compelling your case is, it cannot reach its full potential if it is e-mailed to the wrong group.

How do you devise a mailing list that will garner you more publicity than you know what to do with? You can either develop your own list, buy one, or both. There is even nonprofit software to help you create and maintain a comprehensive mailing list.

The first place to start seems fairly obvious. Start with the people who already support you: your customers. If you do not already have e-mail addresses for them, get them. Request their e-mail on any form you design, whether it is a registration form, a renewal form, an order form, or the like. When they visit your Web site, ask for their e-mail. After all, these are clearly people who want to do business with you and they ought to be your first recipients.

You can also grow your list with a little work. Your Web site is an ideal place to do it quickly and easily. Every page on your site should have a form, or a link to a form, giving visitors the choice to receive your e-mail newsletter. Include an incentive for people who sign up. A free how-to article or white paper often is enough to entice someone to join your list. Note: keep your sign-up form short. You only need a reader's e-mail address at this point. If you must, request their first name so you can personalize communications but resist the urge to get mailing addresses or any other details.

If you do the trade show circuit, have a sign-up sheet available at your booth to capture new names. Be sure your staff knows to direct people's attention to it so it is not overlooked. To encourage more sign-ups, offer a free sample or other enticement.

Some businesses will buy or rent lists. Be wary of this; their quality is likely to be poor when you compare it to the lists you build from your own venues, and a list that is lacking in quality leads to poor response rates. Be that as it may, you could determine that buying or renting lists is the optimal way for you to generate subscribers. Should you decide to purchase a list, understand there is a difference between a list owner and a manager or broker.

A list owner is the organization (or person) that originated the list and maintains it consistently. A list manager is someone who rents several lists from various list owners. A broker is one who charges a fee, or commission, to offer lists from a wider variety of source. Any one of the three should be familiar enough with their lists to help you target the addresses most likely to be receptive to your message.

One quick way to reach a decent-sized audience is to sponsor a list. Find someone who is already sending to the e-mail list you are eyeing and buy a banner ad or pay for a link that will prompt them to join your list. This gives you a targeted audience, reducing the chances of poor response rates. It also can prove to be less expensive than buying a list that may or may not prove effective for you.

As some in the direct mail realm love to say, "Forget mailing more, remember to mail smarter." Then sit back and let the buzz begin!

LEGALESE

When it comes to spam, Uncle Sam has little tolerance. To ensure you are mailing within the letter of the law, familiarize yourself with the CAN-SPAM Act of 2004. The basic rules you need to know are:

1. The "To" and "From" information must be accurate and transparent. Recipients need to know it came from your company.

2. Your subject line needs to match the content of the newsletter. This does not mean you have to be totally conservative; you still can (and should) be creative. Just do not be misleading.

3. Your postal address, not just your e-mail address, must be included in every issue. This speaks to transparency; readers should know how and where to find you outside of the World Wide Web.

4. It has already been mentioned but bears repeating: You must include a way for readers to unsubscribe to your list. It is the law.

A Word of Warning

Remember, though, there is part of the population that either is not Web savvy or does not check e-mail very often. That means you cannot rely on e-mail marketing and newsletters as the sole way to reach out to the public. Consider who you may be excluding if you adopt an online-only policy and think about supplementing your online presence with more traditional marketing means. Your grandmother's advice has never been more appropriate: Resist the urge to put all your eggs in one basket. If you do, you risk being the butt of a lot of yolks in the marketing realm.

AFTER-WORD

- E-mail marketing is a great way to get your message out inexpensively and quickly. You can stay in touch with current clients and reach out to target customers, all while keeping your costs down.

- An e-mail marketing campaign takes a proactive approach. Instead of waiting for people to log on to your Web site to find out what is new, you can let them know almost instantly when you have news to share.

- Opt-in advertising helps you ensure that people who want to be informed about your business get the latest updates. When someone signs up, you know they are interested in your product or service. No more cold calling!

- Even seasonal businesses can benefit from e-mail marketing during their off-season periods. Think about how you can entice customers to give you their business no matter what time of year it is.

- Use easy-to-read fonts and minimal graphics. Let your message stand out, not the packaging. And target your audience carefully. The same e-mail message will not work for all recipients.

- Put a lot of thought into the subject line. This is a lot like making a gourmet meal: presentation is everything. If you can get readers to salivate before even seeing the message, think how they will respond when they get a taste of what you have to say!

- Include a strong and clear call to action so that your readers know what you want them to do in response.

- Implementing an e-mail newsletter or e-zine is a powerful way to build customer loyalty over time. Keep your publications short, targeted, and editorial, with just a hint of promotions for your company to avoid the e-mail marketing feel.

- Regardless of whether you engage in e-mail marketing or an e-newsletter, make sure your mailings meet the legal requirements of the CAN-SPAM Act.

- Start your mailing list with your current customers. Boost it by asking visitors to your Web site to leave their e-mail, and collect e-mail addresses from trade shows or other events. Consider advertising on another business's mailing list as an inexpensive alternative to buying mailing lists from vendors.

A Word From Our Sponsors

Nonprofit organizations stir a passion within their supporters. Whatever the cause — from the environment to children to homelessness or any other topic — the core mission strikes a chord within members who band together to make something happen. They are almost zealous at times because they believe so strongly in the mission.

That is the perfect scenario for word-of-mouth marketing. When people, be they consumers in the marketplace or members of a not-for-profit, feel passionately about something, they share it. That enthusiasm is contagious and it is just one of the reasons that nonprofits especially should be reaping the benefits of the word-of-mouth marketing phenomenon.

This chapter covers:

- Blog and viral marketing for nonprofits

- Nonprofits in virtual reality

- Social networking

- Podcasting

- Cause marketing

- Spokespeople

- Building and maintaining a reputation

NONPROFIT WORD-OF-MOUTH MARKETING

Nonprofits get their own chapter for a few reasons. First, they do not really have a "product" to sell. They have a cause. They have a mission. But they are not centered around something that can be ordered on the Internet. Second, no matter how large they are, they cannot spend advertising dollars to promote their good works the way that for-profits can. For nonprofits, word-of-mouth marketing is a whole different, and critically necessary, beast.

To be sure, elements of word-of-mouth marketing carry over to nonprofits as well as their for-profit counterparts. These organizations require people to talk them up, to share their stories, and to get others jazzed about whatever the cause may be. Certainly not-for-profits can (and should) utilize viral marketing, customer evangelists, and other word-of-mouth tools. At the same time, there are a few tools that may provide better, or at least less expensive, buzz for nonprofits than for corporations. Let us take a look at a couple of them.

BLOGS — AGAIN

Blogs are a natural fit for many types of nonprofits and an excellent way to communicate. Technorati says more than 10,500 blogs include the tags "charity," more than 4,000 are tagged "nonprofit," and nearly 2,300 are tagged with the term "philanthropy." Blogs offer a simple way to reach people and share your message in a noninvasive way. They also enable readers to easily respond to news and actions that may affect your nonprofit, encouraging vital two-way communication that can prove key to building a stronger membership.

The Center for Rural Affairs, a private not-for-profit organization, started the Blog for Rural America and used it to share newspaper articles, Congressional activity, and other pertinent information with those who are passionate about small businesses, family farms, and rural communities.

Blogging is also a terrific fundraising strategy, believe it or not. Oceana, a global science-based nonprofit with a goal to protect the world's oceans, launched a blog as part of its integrated communications strategy. The nonprofit blogs encourage readers to dive in to opportunities to donate or volunteer.

Two words of warning: resist doglish. The phrase "doglish" has been tossed about as the look that your membership gets when you use slang or jargon. Picture the family pooch the last time you said, "Want to take a bath?" An expression of confusion or downright disappointment probably crossed Fido's face. The same is likely to happen if you blog in doglish. Stay away from vague words and mysterious acronyms or risk that your readers will log off quickly to look for the nearest fire hydrant.

CASE STUDY: MAUREEN MCGREGOR

Oceana

2501 M Street, NW

Suite 300

Washington, D.C. 20037

www.oceana.org

202-833-3900 - phone

202-833-2070 - fax

Maureen McGregor - Manager, E-Activism & Marketing

We needed to promote our Cookie Cutter Adoption Program, in which supporters can virtually adopt a marine creature. The adoption "kit" comes with up to 16 ocean-themed cookie cutters, an official adoption certificate, ocean facts, and a special sugar cookie recipe. We also teamed up with Warren Brown, the host of the Food Network's Sugar Rush and founder of the bakery CakeLove.

It is a common practice to highlight fundraising asks throughout an organization's Web site, but a button on the homepage isn't good enough. Blogs often attract an entirely different audience than an organization's regular Web site, so we used our blog to promote the campaign.

We knew it was important to get other bloggers and Web sites to promote our fundraising efforts. We had 2 1/2 full-time staff dedicated to pitching this program to reporters and bloggers, and we built relationships with external contacts throughout the year to get as much visibility as possible. (It is also important to return the favor, promoting other bloggers/Web sites when possible and publicly thanking them for doing a good deed.)

It was surprising how many for-profit companies were willing to donate PSA space, but don't assume that "if you build it, they will come." It is imperative to actively promote your fundraising efforts and not just rely on current supporters.

CASE STUDY: MAUREEN MCGREGOR

If we were to do it all over again, we would have better tracking mechanisms in place to determine which donations resulted from which sources, but we were very pleased with the results. Oceana's 2007 year-end fundraising campaign brought in twice what it did the previous year as a result of our blogging and Web site promotion.

VIRTUAL WORLDS

Create a world with fantastic landscapes and shimmering seas and people will pay to live there, even if it is virtual. They will buy fake land and buildings, faux clothing and cars, and give away real money to actual charities. If it sounds a bit surreal, it is. However, 3-D philanthropy is generating some very big, very real buzz.

Second Life, a fast-growing and virtual community, is an easy place to do it. The site has some 9 million registered users, most of them with avatars (or virtual "selves" of humans). Nonprofits have their own space in this virtual world called the Nonprofit Commons, which is filled to capacity with 32 charitable organizations. (A bit of irony — even in the virtual world there is a waiting list to get in!) The heavily forested Commonwealth Island is another nonprofit haven, where a smattering of real-world donors go to check out what is happening in virtual nonprofit land.

While it all sounds a bit far-fetched, Second Life is bolstering real money for charities. The American Cancer Society has generated all kinds of word of mouth and, in 2007, $115,000 (real dollars, not virtual) in a virtual Relay for Life. Roughly 1,700 avatars "walked" across a 96-acre virtual park in the "Second Life" world. It was a walk-a-thon in cyberspace where no one had to use the restroom and cancer patients could cross the finish line unassisted. It was definitely a buzz campaign with legs.

Save the Children has also benefitted in the real world thanks to the virtual one known as Second Life. Hundreds of people participated in an online 3-D animal pageant called Yak Shack. (Trivia for you: The going rate for yaks in cyberspace is 1,000 Lindens, which translates to about $3.50 in real money.) Once they purchased them, proud cyberyak owners could milk, ride, and care for their virtual beast online in a virtual barn. The charity declined to disclose how much it raised through the stunt, but boasts a raised awareness among a hard-to-reach demographic: youth.

Check out how another not-for-profit organization turned over a new leaf. Plant-It 2020, a nonprofit organization founded by the late singer John Denver, needed to overcome donor fatigue and generate more of an impact for reforestation. The organization partnered with Second Chance Trees, a social media communications initiative, in the real world to stimulate activity in a virtual one. Visitors to the Second Chance Trees Island could purchase and plant a virtual endangered tree for roughly one U.S. real-life dollar. In turn, the purchase triggered the planting of a real tree in an endangered rainforest region including Costa Rica, Brazil, and other environmentally sensitive regions. Those who visited the island learned about the Earth's endangered rainforests while exploring hidden caves, riding along a river, and participating in a multimedia experience about the dangers of deforestation. Plant-It 2020 saw the forest and the trees, and nurtured public awareness of both of them.

VIRAL MARKETING

Viral videos are not limited to the for-profit realm. Nonprofits can benefit from the exposure of forwarded messages too. The same rules apply no matter who is creating a viral piece: It should be short, visually appealing, authentic, and original. That should not keep you from having a little fun with the message, though. On the contrary, the more entertaining you can make it, the farther and faster word of mouth will spread.

World Vision tried its hand at viral marketing for the first time during the 2007 holiday season. The goal for the humanitarian-based nonprofit was to promote its Alternative Gift Catalogue. The viral film spoofed the difficult decision of an affluent British child who was trying to choose whether to have toast or cereal for breakfast. It contrasted his "tough" choice with the lives of the most underprivileged children in the world's poorest countries, trying to cast light on the need to make smart choices that can benefit others all across the globe.

World Vision seeded the viral using YouTube, Google Video, and Joost. The charity also produced a virtual version of the Alternative Gift Catalogue and used Facebook, a social networking site, to encourage gift giving between friends. Results from both campaigns were not available when this book went to press, but if World Vision can see clearly enough to toe dip in the viral and virtual worlds, so can you!

SOCIAL NETWORKING

While the Web-based social networks YouTube, Facebook, and others are relatively new, formal "social networking" has been in use since at least 1892 if not before. Asa Candler, then the owner of Coca-Cola, engaged in social networking — or making contacts through other contacts — to build the soft drink brand. Candler pitched free syrup to pharmacists who would carry Coke, and offered their customers coupons for free drinks. Once a pharmacist agreed to carry his drink, Candler asked each new soda fountain owner to provide him with 128 names of influencers within the community. Why 128? That was the number of ounces of syrup in a gallon of Coca-Cola concentrate.

Candler would mail letters to the 128 people announcing his new product and offering them coupons for a free glass at that pharmacy. Once customers got a taste of Coke, they wanted more. Word of mouth quickly worked its magic and the company soon realized a profit despite the fact that it started by giving away free products. Asa Candler and Coca-Cola are believed to be the first to take advantage of social networking, but today it is easier than ever for businesses and organizations to utilize the many benefits of the practice.

You may be wondering what the short history lesson about Coke and social networking has to do with nonprofits. Without having to give away free inventory, charities are beginning to realize the enormous potential of social networking sites as a free source for donations of money and manpower.

The numbers back that up. According to one study, 15 percent of U.S. Internet users are members of an online community. That may not sound impressive but it gets better. Within that group, 94 percent said the Internet helped educate them about social causes. That is better than Hank Aaron's home run average. (It is also better than my grade in statistics class, which is why I became a writer instead of a statistician.)

The numbers get even more impressive. In 2006, only 30 percent of people said they participated in online communities that had a link to social causes. Yet in just one year, that number jumped to 75 percent. In 2007, three out of four people had some kind of tie to a Web-based social cause network.

If your nonprofit is not yet taking advantage of this explosive growth, it is certainly worth investigating the opportunity to get your message out there in a newer and more dynamic way. As time goes by, you have more options. First, there was MySpace, but before long, Facebook, Xanga, MSN Spaces, and Yahoo! Groups were born, along with a host of others. Any of these has the potential of helping your nonprofit grow and thrive.

Beyond being a place to meet and connect with friends online, MySpace has become involved with charitable platforms. One included promoting Product Red, an economic initiative that aims to help combat AIDS in Africa. In addition, the site launched a new channel dedicated to social causes. Called MySpace Impact, it lets users start campaigns, offer to volunteer their time, and raise funds on behalf of charities.

Competitor social network Facebook has partnered with different not-for-profits, first creating virtual icons for breast cancer research. For a dollar apiece, users purchased images of anything from a birthday cake to a can labeled "whoop ass." The net proceeds were donated through e-philanthropy to the research charity Komen for the Cure. Later, Facebook launched a holiday giving initiative on behalf of UNICEF, with a gift icon carrying a heftier price tag of $17 to help save a child's life through immunizations, and Save the Children which let users group together to make donations. Facebook users also have the option to register for Causes, which enables members to create a cause and raise money through the application that is then given to a registered charity.

But not-for-profit organizations need not wait for the sites to offer a partnership. Simply by creating a profile on the social networking sites, nonprofits can immediately gain access to an unlimited number of potential "friends," a list of their interests, and a forum to generate discussion and promotion. A 2006 study shows that 55 percent of online American youths use online social networking sites. While the 12 to 17 age group may not be the first place nonprofits will turn to for support, the teens perhaps represent a future trend; as they age, they will likely continue to connect on these sites. Also, research has shown that today's youth is more volunteer oriented than previous generations — and what nonprofit organization can afford to turn away volunteer power?

The Humane Society of the United States has used both Facebook and MySpace for advocacy and fundraising. The country's most powerful animal welfare organization has found success in both community building and advocacy participation. Carie Lewis, the Humane Society's Internet Marketing Manager, shared some of her most important lessons learned while social networking:

1. **Create a cause.** That means create something specific for a campaign instead of just a general cause for your organization. People are more motivated by a particular event or platform than they are by generic missions.

2. **Update your content regularly.** If you create a group and then ignore it, the group will fizzle and you will not reap any benefits. If you foster the group, though, and provide fresh content and reasons for people to get involved, you

can see an increase in participation and hopefully in donations.

3. **Listen and react.** Monitor what people are saying about issues related to your mission, and use your social networking group to express your organization's position. It helps establish you as an authority and constantly reminds people of your presence and your goals.

4. **Converse.** Yes, that means "respond" in online speak. If someone replies to your response, answer them. People want to know they were heard and if they do not hear back from you, they will assume you did not listen to them.

5. **Build your member's network by promoting your organization's profile and adding your social network links to your Web site.** Keep an eye on the "causes" area of each network and reach out to new members or new causes. Social networking is very much based on word of mouth; when people see you listed in their friends' groups, they are more likely to join your group too.

The Allstate Foundation, an independent charitable organization, created "Keep the Drive," a teen-to-teen movement based on peer influence. The goal was to help teens make responsible choices, both behind the wheel and in the passenger seat, and share their commitment with others. Allstate built a Web site and created a custom profile on MySpace, featuring an open forum, a comment section, and a safe driving quiz. Within the first month of the campaign, the MySpace profile attracted nearly 900 friends and received more than 28,000 unique visits. Profile visitors averaged four page views, indicating they were actively engaged and not just making a pit stop. Clearly, teens felt they were in good hands on Allstate's social networking page.

WIDGETS

While Widget was a character in Marvel Comics as well as a '90s animated TV show, widgets have a special place in the world of the Web. They are personalized updates you can choose to put on your computer, including weather information, Web cams, games, scoreboards, calendars, and radio stations, among others. At this point, you are probably wondering why you are reading about these gizmos in the non-profit chapter of a book on word-of-mouth marketing. It is because widgets were instrumental in helping Music for Relief, a charitable organization, raise much-needed awareness and funds.

The not-for-profit was trying to raise money to help the victims of the California wildfires in 2007, with little success. Young people did not have the money to donate and did not have any way to spread the word about the charity to those who could afford to help. Music for Relief wanted to accomplish two things: increase awareness and donations made on its Web site.

When a widget vendor offered to work for free to create and add a widget poll to the site, it was music to the nonprofit's ears. Music for Relief added a widget to its own Web site, its MySpace page, and on the Web site of is its founding members, Linkin Park. The widget took the form of a poll, offering respondents a chance to win items from everything like tickets and VIP passes to an autographed instrument or a signed poster. The widget was created to be easily added to any users' Web sites as well as shared with other viewers. It worked.

Hundreds of MySpace users and bloggers added the poll widget to their personal sites and ultimately raised thousands of dollars for the relief effort. Music for Relief saw donations increase by 20 percent and well more than 18,000 participants took the poll and included it on their individual MySpace pages. Not a bad return on investment for the fundraising effort.

There are those that doubt the future of the social networking sites due to privacy concerns, deception online, and more sites charging for the privilege of connecting. Despite the skeptics, this social revolution can be a Godsend for grassroots groups and nonprofit organizations, helping them increase their visibility and gather information on potential donors without dropping a dime on big marketing budgets.

You may find that social networks will not work for your nonprofit, and there is nothing wrong with that. Nevertheless, you should at least consider the idea. It does not require a technical wizard or a 'Net guru. Successful social networking does require a commitment of both time and patience. You will need to cultivate a group and keep your discussion boards current to keep people engaged. When you do, though, you open the door to an unlimited number of potential supporters, members, and donors. And if that does not strike you as nonprofit nirvana, it is hard to imagine what does.

PODCASTING

This term makes me think of the sci-fi flick *Invasion of the Body Snatchers*, but it definitely does more good than the pod people featured in the movie, who work together to kill off the entire human race. Podcasting, in a nutshell, involves creating audio or video programs that can be downloaded and viewed via computers or MP3s. It can include talk shows, tutorials, or other audio content. Think of it as a way to share audio files with the world the same way you would share your annual report with your membership.

The benefits are pretty clear: nonprofits can create a low-cost product to share with a potentially world-wide audience. All you need are some basic recording tools, including a microphone, some free software, and a fast Internet connection. It is easy to update and change podcasts without spending money to preprint and distribute more mainstream media materials. Plus, no matter how well-written the copy is, there is a human element to seeing or hearing someone share their cause that is often lost in the written word.

Podcasts can even become sources for donations. Jason Calacanis of America Online created a podcast and offered sponsorship on his blog, promising that all revenue would go to fund scholarships for inner city students in Brooklyn. Two sponsors, GoDaddy and PodTech.net, anted up fees totaling $100,000. The donations covered the costs for two kids without the means to attend the school. Ironically, Calacanis himself originally pooh-poohed the idea of podcasts, saying the technology would never catch on.

Who can you reach with a podcast? An October 2006 comScore study found that half of all podcast listeners are between 35 and 54 years old, an audience broader than many previously thought. A majority — 63 percent — are male. And those with a household income of at least $100,000 annually are 28 percent more likely than the average Internet user to download podcasts. With a broad audience and a growing following, podcasting is a dynamic new way for nonprofits to reach supporters and constituents.

As with most things in life, there are a few guidelines to follow, though:

1. Keep podcasts short, especially as you are trying them for the first time.

2. Stay focused on one topic for each podcast.

3. Keep them awake! Make the podcaster's voice warm and personal, nothing too "preachy" or disinterested.

4. Always identify your podcast at the beginning with the date, the topic, and the guest. It will help keep both you and your listeners from getting confused.

5. Keywords are every bit as important in podcasts as they are in Web sites. Use appropriate and relevant keywords in your feed's title and description so listeners will find your cast.

One of the most compelling guidelines needs to be called out all on its own. Make it easy for people to get your podcasts. Include subscriber links on your nonprofit's blog or Web site so listeners know where to find the newest editions. With podcasting, online publishers create something called an RSS feed, which can automatically download a podcast as soon as it is available, and it is almost immediate. Subscribers can receive your podcasts without having to log on and look for them on your Web site; like email, a podcast is delivered any time of the day or night.

As a nonprofit, you depend on the press to help you get publicity. Podcasts are press-release friendly. Distribute a press release about your upcoming cast to editors and free online press release directories so you can let the newshounds know what you are up to.

One final note: Remember that podcasting — like word-of-mouth marketing — is still a relatively new technology and not everyone understands how to use it. As a nonprofit, it is an invaluable and inexpensive way to share your message, but it will only help you if your audience knows how to access it. Educate your constituents if they are not a technical bunch so that they can get the most out of this growing medium for buzz marketing.

Being a nonprofit does not exclude you from sharing your message in a dynamic way. One of my favorite emails came from the editor of *Chesapeake Family* magazine. I had just finished writing my first freelance article for them and I got an email with the subject line, "Thanks." I expected the standard comments to follow, something along the line of "We appreciate your efforts and hope to work with you again" or some other such sleep-inducing verbiage. Instead, the body of the email said, "... for not SUCKING." Just like that! I laughed so hard I think I snorted diet Coke out of my nose. (Note to self: Turn head away from keyboard before doing that again.) Turned out the editor had had some problems with other freelancers who were late with an assignment or did not adequately cover the subject matter. She was grateful I could listen and follow directions, and that was her message, but instead of the standard way to say it, she sure did catch my attention. I even saved the email just to make me grin from time to time.

Clearly, that example is not appropriate for most email marketing campaigns. I simply use it to illustrate that email does not have to be as dry as saltine crackers. In fact, the more staid and conservative you are, the less word-of-mouth marketing can accomplish. But if you are willing to take a chance and try something a bit more daring, you are more likely to spark some buzz.

That is what GRACE, the GrassRoots Action Center for the Environment, did when it commissioned Free Range Studios to create The Meatrix, an award-winning short Adobe Flash film. The point was to encourage consumers to purchase organic foods and free-range meats. If you have not seen it for yourself, do a quick Google search and behold the powerful impact of this nonprofit's message. Had the point been made in a standard email or podcast, the result could have been muddier than a pig in a puddle, but because GRACE was daring enough to be creative, more than 15 million people have been exposed to its message about the dangers of industrial agriculture. It was so popular that two sequels were produced to further the point. When was the last time your nonprofit was able to reach that many donors?

PUBLICITY STUNTS

Just because you are a nonprofit, you are not exempt from sharing your mission in an eye-catching way. The international humanitarian organization Médecins du Monde pulled off an extremely clever and altruistic grassroots marketing campaign in 2005. The French brand of the organization wanted to draw attention to the plight of the homeless people in Paris, so it created the "tent city" initiative. The group gave out approximately 300 tents — each emblazoned with the Médicins du Monde logo — to destitute Parisians sleeping outside. When the homeless gathered together along the Quai d'Austerlitz and the Canal

Saint-Martin, the public became intimately aware of just how many homeless people resided in the area and the reaction was swift. Public outcry forced a rare off-season government session, where officials admitted that Paris's homeless shelters were hugely overcrowded. Millions of dollars were immediately allocated for emergency housing and Médicins du Monde received some valuable word of mouth.

Goodwill of Greater Washington hosts an annual fashion show featuring vintage and contemporary clothing available at Goodwill retail stores. It is timed to coincide with the launch of fashion week in New York City and is designed to make the nonprofit's retail stores more appealing to young professionals. After a few successful years, Goodwill took its stunt to a world-wide audience by launching a virtual runway show and online auction in 2007, garnering attention from media including *PRWeek* and *The Chronicle of Philanthropy*. The show featured items for sale on Goodwill's eBay site and drew more than 600 readers a week in the first six weeks, retaining more than 25 percent of readers and converting better than three percent of visitors into online Goodwill shoppers. Not bad for selling items that were donated in the first place! Users saw the outfits, watched the show, got jazzed about the deals to be had, and started talking about it.

Remember, though, when it comes to publicity stunts, you will need to ensure that people associate your nonprofit and its message with the activity. You will not benefit if the public remembers the stunt but forgets that your association was behind it. How many interesting ads have you seen that leave you remembering the ad but forgetting the product? The same holds true when it comes to events. In the example above, Goodwill used the event to educate the public about its mission of job training for the disadvantaged and disabled. Carefully craft a must-see event but keep your message and your organization at the forefront — or risk being lost in the crowd of onlookers.

CAUSE MARKETING

Nonprofits have the luxury of joining forces with for-profits and sharing their marketing dollars in what is called cause marketing, or sometimes referred to as strategic philanthropy. Corporations are suffering from a crisis of consumer confidence and, as a result, are more interested in building credibility and connecting with influencers in a local, human way. There is a good reason for that: one of three U.S. college students plunk down their hard-earned cash on brands that give back to the community, are environmentally safe, or are connected to a cause. The pairing of for-profits and not-for-profits can take the form of promoting a common message, product endorsement, or partnering for a cause.

You may not think of not-for-profits when it comes to product endorsement but it happens. Picture the American Heart Association giving Cheerios and the Florida Department of Citrus certification for being heart healthy. The association even formed a relationship with the National Cattlemen's Beef Association to promote lean cuts of beef. However, you will not find many nonprofits willing to engage in product endorsement, for the very fact that it can appear as though they are only endorsing it for the money regardless of its advantages. However, if, as a nonprofit, you find that you can endorse something with a clear conscience, it can bring you much-needed visibility.

Partnerships are also popular in cause marketing. Yoplait yogurt launched the Save Lids to Save Lives campaign on behalf of the Susan G. Komen Breast Cancer Foundation. Yoplait produces containers with a pink lid, and for each lid that consumers turn in, the company donates ten cents to the nonprofit. The partnerships extend beyond yogurt, though. In 2004, The Home Depot and the American Red Cross formed a partnership called Ready Gear designed to educate one million people on hurricane and disaster preparedness. Needless to say, when a nonprofit can link to a corporation to maximize funds and share its message, it benefits all parties involved. The not-for-profit gets valuable visibility and income and the corporation enjoys greater social responsibility.

Following the disastrous Hurricane Katrina, Proctor and Gamble teamed up with the St. Bernard Project, a grassroots organization providing support to those in the St. Bernard Parish in New Orleans. The detergent company started its efforts with Tide CleanStart, washing more than 20,000 loads of laundry with its mobile laundry program. The service began offering free laundry services after Katrina devastated many families in the Gulf Coast region. In 2007, the program expanded its reach to San Diego to assist families and firefighters affected by the wide-spread wildfires there. It also designed a vintage-style T-shirt to sell to help raise more funds for the effort.

Sometimes the beneficiaries are youth. Target's Take Charge of Education program has donated millions to the nation's schools in the ten years since it began. Crest partnered with Boys & Girls Clubs of America to promote health, fitness, and recreation.

Other times, the environment is the cause. In 1998, General Mills joined with The Nature Conservancy for a cause-related marketing program for Nature Valley Granola Bars, securing editorials in Newsweek magazine and devoting space on product packaging for environmental messages about rainforest preservation and river restoration.

In each case, no matter who partnered with whom, the nonprofit's message was spread much wider than it could have been on its own, and the corporation involved boosted its credibility and its sales.

It would be ideal if your local community nonprofit could pick up the phone and immediately pair up with Nabisco or Nike but that is about as likely as Goliath calling David and inviting him for a cup of coffee at the local Starbucks. It is merely a matter of scale. Nonprofits can work with local companies to further cause marketing as long as they target a corporation carefully. But how do you do that?

If you are a nonprofit looking to establish a business partnership to help spread word of mouth about your mission, there are three things to ask yourself:

1. **Does my cause match their demographic?** If you are a nonprofit focused on under-served children, partnering with a local grocery store makes sense. Joining forces with a tobacco retailer does not.

2. **Can I offer them brand visibility?** Sponsors are not as likely to agree to a partnership if they are going to be one of dozens of corporations named; they like to be front and center. Be sure you can offer them some unique opportunities to showcase their brand.

3. **What is in it for them?** Make sure that your targeted company understands what they will get out of the

partnership. In addition to creating goodwill within your community, you should point out potential increases in response rates and traffic to their Web site as well as ROI (return on investment). It would be nice if businesses wanted to do the right thing for the sake of doing the right thing, but they are more likely to be motivated by their bottom line.

THE EFFECT OF SPOKESPEOPLE

Joining forces with a celebrity spokesperson can help generate word of mouth for your nonprofit organization. They have a built-in fan base with whom to share your message and have access to countless media outlets to further generate buzz.

The first thing to consider when selecting a celebrity to help your nonprofit is a personal connection — who has a natural tie-in to your cause? Who is affected by your mission? A celebrity who feels passionate about what you are doing is every bit as powerful as a customer evangelist, and they have the mouthpiece to shout your name across the globe. One who is not at all involved in your particular mission will be less than effective; they could, in fact, be a total turnoff, which can prove devastating to a word-of-mouth campaign.

There are a few words of caution regarding celebrity spokespeople, however. Fame is fleeting, so choose wisely. Be sure the star you choose has staying power before you put all of your eggs in their diamond-encrusted basket.

Also, we have seen far too many stories of celebrities gone wild. Even stars who seem stable and respectable occasionally get in hot water with the public or the law. What would you do if the headlines take your spokesperson down? Be prepared, just in case.

How to Build and Maintain a Reputation

From fundraiser letters to crisis communication, not-for-profit organizations have myriad opportunities to build a strong reputation. People like to support companies and causes they feel are trustworthy. Smart management, good deeds, and great volunteers can go a long way toward creating and maintaining a positive public image.

But it does not happen overnight. Automaker Henry Ford once said, "You cannot build a reputation on what you are going to do." It takes time for people to develop trust, just as it takes repeated exposure to positive word of mouth for the public to believe what they are hearing. Be consistent, be patient, and be buzz-worthy. Let people know what you are doing to make a difference. Invite them to witness your good works first-hand by volunteering to be part of the solution. Remember, people like to feel like they are a part of a team. Giving them good reason to become involved is an excellent way to accomplish that. And never give them reason to question your motives.

Keeping that in mind, here are tips to building a good reputation and a few ways to cope if some negative buzz tarnishes it.

Fundraiser Letters

Most nonprofits rely on their donors to keep their doors open and nothing is more crucial than a well-written fundraiser letter. A heartfelt plea with specific examples can entice a donor to become a lifelong giver. On the flip side, a generic, fill-in-the-blank-type missive is too generic to be effective. You may convince someone to be a one-time donor, but your goal should be to inspire them to become a sort of customer evangelist who will help you shout your mission from the rooftops. Make your fundraiser letter come alive with emotional language and a strong call to action so that donors feel compelled to act, not just in the form of a donation but as a mouthpiece for your mission. After all, money will not spread word of mouth — people will.

Testimonials

Ah, there it is again, that word. It crops up nearly as often as crabgrass but it sure is more pleasing when viewed from a word-of-mouth perspective. When your nonprofit holds an event to make a difference in your community or helps someone in need, ask those who you have assisted to tell people about it. It may sound like tooting your own horn, and perhaps it is, but it is an excellent way to build trust, good will, and a strong reputation for doing good deeds, all of which are essential to creating buzz. A terrific bonus: You have more control over testimonials than you do actual conversations between people, enabling you to hone your message or utilize them in the best possible place.

Testimonials feed so beautifully into word-of-mouth marketing that it is impossible to ignore them, and yet, it is amazing how many nonprofits do not put them to good use. Testimonials provide prospective members, donors, volunteers, and stakeholders with a human face, a good story, and an objective opinion — the very basis of a word-of-mouth campaign. Should you find your nonprofit in a not-so-pleasant light, pull out every good thing that anyone has ever said about your work. Be sure to include the name and title of the person to underscore the credibility.

A word of note: Gather testimonials whenever possible, especially following a big event or gathering of your membership. Sprinkle them like confectioner's sugar wherever you can: on your Web site, in your brochure, and any other marketing materials you can think of. It would be a mistake to pull them out only in a negative publicity situation. Utilize this available and very powerful tool at every turn — it is a self-promoting word-of-mouth campaign.

Online Reputation Management

With the Internet, it is much easier for people to say things about your nonprofit in a much more public setting. It is also harder for you to manage your reputation with the whole world having access to their comments. Here are some basic, easy-to-follow tips for online reputation management:

- Get online as often as you can and review every post you can find that mentions your nonprofit. Sign up for an online service that alerts you each time you get mentioned.

- Answer every post. Good or bad, it does not matter. It is simply a courtesy (as well as smart public relations) to let posters know that you heard them, even if you did not like what they said.

- Thank the people who say good things about your organization — they are hugely important to your positive word of mouth. Invite them to share their views with as many people as possible.

- If you find someone who is unhappy with your charity, find out why. You can do this privately or online, but at least acknowledge their post publicly so that others see you are being proactive. Otherwise it may appear you have stuck your head in the sand to avoid seeing any negative press.

- Unhappy posters hold a unique opportunity for you, believe it or not. If you can convince them to give you another chance, you can actually change their mind. Convert a nay-sayer and you have just upped your positive word of mouth immeasurably.

- Encourage (but do not pay!) your membership to post favorable things about your charity. After all, these are your supporters. Who better to help you spread some good WOM?

Crisis Management

Even the best-intentioned nonprofits could potentially find themselves in adverse situations with the media. This is where it is crucial to manage negative buzz as we will discuss further in Chapter 11. A few words specific to nonprofits are appropriate here, though. Should you find yourself in the unenviable position of trying to explain an action that has generated negative word of mouth, there are a few things to keep in mind.

Develop a clear message that is concise and honest. Craft a statement that showcases the positive works in which your nonprofit has engaged and be certain that it underscores your mission. Do not ever try to cover up or lie about a situation in which your organization has made a mistake; the truth will come out and your credibility will be forever dinged if not destroyed. Instead, if your organization was in the wrong, admit to it and lay out the ways in which you will respond differently in the future. Most people are willing to forgive someone who requests it but they will not forget a lie.

Designate an experienced spokesperson. Be sure that your designated professional is trained to provide an appropriate response to negative publicity. It can be nerve-wracking enough to be in front of a microphone, but when the questions being asked imply wrongdoing or mismanagement, it is imperative that a representative can keep his or her cool under the pressure. A key reminder: Ensure that every member of your organization, including your volunteers, knows who is designated to handle the media and that they are the only person qualified to answer questions. Just as too many cooks in the kitchen can ruin a good stew, too many people responding to negative publicity can mar the chance to overcome bad press.

One example of extremely well-handled crisis management is Johnson & Johnson's handling of the Tylenol scare. In 1982, the product was tampered with, resulting in the deaths of seven people. A widespread panic followed as people tried to determine how many products were laced with cyanide and how far the tampering had spread. The company suffered a whale of a blow in its market value.

When the same thing happened again in 1986, Johnson & Johnson knew how to react. Having weathered the earlier crisis, it immediately recalled all Tylenol from store shelves, not just the outlets in the state where it had been tampered with. It announced that the product would not be restocked until the company designed tamper-proof packaging so that it could not happen again.

The crisis hit the company hard in the wallet. Beyond the initial impact on Wall Street, Johnson & Johnson lost big bucks due to lost production and destroyed goods as a result of the recall. However, it gained considerable consumer trust for acting quickly and decisively, and for going beyond what was necessary to ensure public safety. There is some evidence that consumers actually changed to the Tylenol brand following the incident because they were reassured by the steps the manufacturer had taken. By handling the situation quickly, acknowledging responsibility, and offering empathy, Johnson & Johnson turned the tide of public opinion.

AFTER-WORD

- Like their for-profit counterparts, nonprofits can benefit from blogs, viral and email marketing, and other word-of-mouth tools. Charities can also reap the benefits of some nontraditional ways to build buzz, like virtual worlds.

- Social networks like YouTube and Facebook provide a potent pool of prospective members. When used correctly, they can be a source of donations, both of the monetary and volunteer kind.

- Create a specific cause for social networking to increase participation. People may be more likely to give to a one-time special event than to a general nonprofit fund.

- Podcasting is a low-cost way to create a message to share

with the world. Podcasts are easily and quickly created and updated so nonprofits can highlight their needs on an on-going basis without the expense of producing and mailing reports and requests.

- If you create a podcast, keep it simple, engaging, and identifiable. Make it easy for people to get it and to share it to maximize your word-of-mouth potential.

- Publicity stunts can help not-for-profit organizations generate fantastic word of mouth. Be sure your stunt is centered on your message so people remember both what they saw and who initiated it; otherwise, it will fail to net your organization any new members.

- Cause marketing is a phenomenal way for nonprofits and for-profits to collaborate to maximize resources. By relying on a partner's dollars and visibility, a charity can spread its message farther than it could alone.

- Spokespeople can help generate buzz for a nonprofit, thanks to a built-in fan base and access to media outlets. Be sure to choose a celebrity who is personally connected in some way to your cause and select someone who likely has some staying power so that your charity's flame does not get extinguished when their limelight dims.

- Build a reputation based on consistency, accountability, and good word of mouth. Use testimonials from clients you have helped or other partners who have witnessed your mission at work.

- Should you find your charity suffering from a ding to its reputation, develop a clear message that showcases what you have done right and acknowledges what went wrong. Choose an experienced spokesperson to deliver the message so there are no conflicting accounts of what happened or what is being done to correct it.

THE F-WORD

GET your mind out of the gutter: The title of this chapter, "The F-Word," is not what you are thinking. This is a chapter about ethics in WOM, so in this case, "F" stands for "F-alse." Or "F-ake." Or "F-ony." That may be stretching it a bit, but you get the idea. Misleading marketing is unacceptable and can undo a successful word-of-mouth campaign faster than technology changes.

What is more, you are about to discover that you do not need to mislead the public. With an already-skeptical public who is wary of traditional marketing, being honest and transparent is a breath of fresh air and can actually win you more customers. Who knew that the phrase "the F-word" could also mean "F-orthright?"

This chapter covers:

- Ethics in word-of-mouth marketing

- WOMMA's 20 ethics questions

- Why transparency is crucial

- Blogola

Keeping It Real

Of course, someone has to be the ethics police and that would be part of my job. I could not write an entire book on word-of-mouth marketing and not include something about how to use it responsibly, and that is something that sets this book apart. There are other books about buzz campaigns, many of them with great content, but most either do not mention ethics at all, or at most, give it a passing mention. I believe the subject warrants an entire chapter.

Honest marketing may sound like an oxymoron, in the same category as jumbo shrimp, but it behooves businesses to be transparent in buzz campaigns. Any time you try to pull the wool over people's eyes, it will come back to haunt you. Either sales suffer, credibility gets damaged, or both happen, and the end result is disastrous. So, as painful as it may be, please read through this. It is worth your time to spare yourself losing marketing money — not to mention lost credibility — after a flubbed campaign.

Nearly 90 percent of those participating in a 2005-2006 study on word of mouth responded that it is an ethical form of marketing. The study showed which practices are deemed most unethical and the clear winner (or loser) was hiring incentivized agents from a third party to post product reviews on blogs or message boards. A whopping 75 percent of respondents agreed that paying someone to appear to be casually interested in a product or service is dead wrong. The survey also stressed that organizations that are now using or considering using word-of-mouth campaigns should never use minors to help spread the word. Check out the Dr. Pepper example below to find out why that is a huge faux pas.

Two other methods were also strongly perceived as unethical. Most of us have probably experienced the first: a company that sends unsolicited emails to customers. I do not know about you, but I immediately delete them and they definitely leave a taste worse than morning breath in my mouth. That is certainly not the impression you want to give people of your business, especially when it is remarkably ineffective in resulting in sales.

The other practice that respondents felt strongly about involves incentives. The survey referenced above showed nearly 62 percent think it is unethical to get people who are not using a product or service, but are on a company's mailing list, to talk about them by giving them something in return.

But wait — earlier in this book, we discussed using incentives as a way to get people more fired up about spreading the word. So, what is okay and what is not? The difference is that it is all right to give people incentives to talk about a product or service that they are already using. It is not ethical to incentivize people who do not know a thing about whether the product or service is worth its salt. See the difference?

Word of Mouth Marketing Association Toolkit

Ethics are such an important issue that the Word of Mouth Marketing Association created a Practical Ethics Toolkit in 2006. It is a series of 20 questions to help marketers identify and squelch unethical tactics before finding themselves up some well-known stinky creek without a paddle.

Honesty of Relationship

1. Do we insist that our advocates always disclose their relationship with us — including all forms of compensation, incentives, or samples?

Honesty of Opinion

1. Do we insist that all opinions shared with the public express the honest and authentic opinion of the consumer or advocate without manipulation or falsification?

2. Are those individuals who are speaking for us free to form their own opinions and share all feedback, including negative feedback?

3. Is all of the information provided to advocates, consumers, and the media factual and honest, and are all of our claims accurate?

Honesty of Identity

1. Have we repudiated and forbidden all forms of shill, stealth, and undercover marketing?

2. Does everyone working on our behalf use their true identity and disclose their affiliation with our company and agencies?

3. Do we forbid the blurring of identification in ways that might confuse or mislead consumers as to the true identity of the individuals with whom they are communicating?

4. Do we forbid the use of expressly deceptive practices

from our employees/advocates, such as impersonating consumers; concealing their true identities; or lying about factors such as age, gender, race, familiarity with or use of product, or other circumstances intended to enhance the credibility of the advocate while deliberately misleading the public?

Taking Responsibility

1. If we use agents or volunteers of any sort, do we actively instruct them in ethical practices and behaviors and insist that all of those working under our instructions similarly comply with this standard?

2. Do we instruct all advocates to repeat these instructions and responsibilities in the downstream conversation?

3. Do we have a plan to monitor any inappropriate word of mouth generated by our advocates?

4. Do we know how we will correct any inappropriate or unethical word of mouth done by volunteers or resulting from actions taken by us?

5. Do we insist that campaign organizers disclose their involvement when asked by consumers or the media and provide contact information upon request?

Respecting the Rules

1. Do we respect and honor the rules of any media we might use, including all such procedures and stipulations as may be deemed appropriate by specific Web sites, blogs,

discussion forums, traditional media, or live events? (Examples of actions that break the rules: violating the terms of service of any online site, spamming, violating privacy rules, or defacing public property.)

2. Do we prohibit all word of mouth programs involving children aged 13 and younger?

3. If our campaign involves communicating with or influencing minors aged 14 to 17, do we a) have mechanisms in place to protect the interests of those teens, and b) have parental notification mechanisms in place, where appropriate?

When Hiring an Agency

1. Does the agency subscribe to the same high standards of ethical behavior and practice, and are they willing to guarantee the ethics of their own work as well as that of all subcontractors?

2. Do they have reporting and operational review procedures in place permitting us to ensure full compliance with all ethical standards?

3. Have they previously engaged in unethical practices?

4. If they have ever engaged in such practices in the past, do they now prohibit them, and will they guarantee that they will not use employees who have engaged in fraudulent practices to work on our behalf?

As an extra measure of assurance, ask yourself:

- Would I be uncomfortable if my family or friends were involved in this campaign?

- Is there anything about this campaign that we would be embarrassed to discuss publicly?

WOMMA calls the basic concept behind the Ethics Code the "Honesty ROI." It is based on honesty of Relationship, Opinion, and Identity.

- **Honesty of Relationship:** say who you are speaking for

- **Honesty of Opinion:** say what you truly believe; you never shill

- **Honesty of Identity:** say who you are; never falsify or hide your identity

The association even created a great saying that bears repeating over and over:

"Remember: Consumers come first, honesty is not optional, and deception is always exposed."

Effects of Unethical Campaigns

Deception can be devastating to a buzz campaign. At the very least, credibility, trust, and confidence in a company are compromised, and it takes a long time to regain those. In a worst-case scenario, misleading or other unethical practices can put a business out of business, quickly or over time. Whatever the result may be, receiving and recovering from negative word of mouth is clearly not worth the risk taken by trying to mislead the public.

The social networking site Facebook learned that the hard way when it tried to track what its users were doing on other partner Web sites and report it back to the users' Facebook friends. (If that is too confusing to you, just suffice it to say that Facebook was playing tattle-tale.) The goal was to give participating online companies a way to monitor what Facebook users were doing on their site and to use that information to target messages to their friends. Spying and tattling at the same time. That is almost as bad as wearing white after Labor Day (except that only makes you look uncouth, not dishonest).

If you still have trouble comprehending why this is so bad, take this example: Facebook collaborates with a third party, such as Overstock.com. A Facebook user buys a big, diamond ring from Overstock. With Beacon in place, Facebook immediately knows that its member bought that particular "bling" and includes that information in the member's News Feed.

When the user is checking out at Overstock, he or she sees a popup ad, asking if it is okay to let the users' friends know about their newest purchase. Say the user is a guy who is buying an engagement ring as a surprise for his beloved, so he declines to have that information published for the world to see.

There is the rub. It turns out that Facebook was still collecting and sending the information even when users said no.

To make an icky situation even worse, Facebook made multiple mistakes in the Beacon brouhaha. One, the site was not forthcoming about what it was doing. Many users had no clue that the information was being collected in the first place. In other words, they did not understand just how much of their privacy was being invaded.

Second, Facebook's Beacon ad service made it difficult to opt out of the program. According to some security researchers (Computer Associates Inc.), Beacon continued to track the activities of users even after they had logged off from Facebook and declined the option of having their activities on other sites broadcast back to their friends. Facebook gave the impression that it was allowing people to keep some information private when it was still up to the same old tricks.

Being above-board is tantamount to credibility, whether you are authoring a blog or just responding to one. In researching this book, I came across a blog-alogue (I just made that word up — it is what I call a dialogue within in a blog) about Charity Navigator. The tool helps evaluate the financial health of the largest charities in the United States so that donors can more easily choose to whom they want to give their hard-earned cash. One post from "Elie" trashed the tool, saying that it only looks at the percentage of an organization's expenses that go to overhead versus programs. His point was that Charity Navigator does not disclose what the programs are or how they work.

One person responded to Elie's post, saying, "Just should point out Elie is hardly a disinterested party as a principal of Givewell" (another organization that helps donors earmark the best possible charity for their donation). Now, I had never heard of either of these organizations before, but I immediately had a bad taste in my mouth about Givewell, simply because Elie did not disclose his affiliation with the nonprofit before slamming someone else. Had he mentioned that he was working with Givewell, it would not have bothered me at all that he expressed a negative opinion. After all, who does not dislike their competition? But because his affiliation was only revealed by a third party, his post made me wonder what else his organization might be hiding. I am not saying they are dishonest — I am simply pointing out that my first impression of Givewell was negative, all because of a lack of transparency.

One of the most devastating results of negative word of mouth is consumer boycotting of the company or product. For decades, the Nestle Corporation has found itself at the center of a boycott for reportedly violating the World Health Assembly marketing requirements. The company markets its breast milk substitute to nursing mothers worldwide, including Third World and developing countries. Consumer backlash maintains that Nestle is making a profit off its product while encouraging impoverished families to switch to formula. The company has stayed in business despite years of consumer boycotting but the damage to both its reputation and its bottom line continues to cost the company dearly.

Dr. Pepper can relate. In 2003, the company was introducing Raging Cow, a new milk-based beverage and offered a group of bloggers some incentives to discuss the product online. The soft-drink manufacturer asked the bloggers not to discuss that they had been briefed on the product. Care to guess what happened? Someone snitched and bloggers revolted, calling for a boycott. Never heard of Raging Cow? Now you know why.

There is even a term for fake blogs, also known as flogs. Weblogs that are seemingly grassroots but really backed by a business or political group are referred to as "astroturfing." Love Astroturf? Do your blogging on **www.asgoodasgrass.com**, and leave the real opines to real people.

A WORD **A**BOUT **A**GENTS

So, what happens if a company uses an agent to engage in word-of-mouth marketing? Does that automatically turn off a prospective buyer? Not at all, according to the "To Tell or Not to Tell?" report conducted by Northeastern University. The study was conducted to determine whether disclosing corporate affiliation had any practical advantages or any drawbacks.

The full study is available at **www.waltercarl.neu.edu/downloads** but here is a summary of the main findings:

Roughly 75 percent of the conversational partners did not mind talking with someone affiliated with a marketing organization. It was more important to them they trusted the agent was providing an honest opinion, felt the agent had their best interests at heart, and the agent was providing relevant and valuable information.

The agent volunteered his or her affiliation with the marketing organization without being prompted 75 percent of the time.

When an agent disclosed his or her affiliation up front, it had no impact on the key outcome metrics (credibility, inquiry, use, purchase, and pass-along/relay). In fact, just the opposite happened. For instance, when the conversational partner was aware they were talking with a participant in an organized word-of-mouth marketing campaign, the pass-along/relay rate (the number of people a person told after speaking with a word-of-mouth agent) actually increased.

When the customer had already heard about a product before speaking with a marketing agent, the initial source of information had more credibility. In more than 75 percent of the cases where the conversational partners had learned about a brand or product from another source of information (such as print, radio, TV, or Web advertisement), talking with a marketing agent increased the believability of the first source. Agent disclosure did not change that, either.

Contrast that with the fallout that happened when people were not aware of the agent's affiliation with the marketing association. For about 5 percent of the conversational partners, there was a negative "backlash" effect when they learned that the agent was connected to the organization. These negative feelings took different forms. Sometimes, the negative feelings were directed toward the agent or the interaction with that agent. More importantly, that negativity was sometimes directed at the brand being discussed, and the company who made the brand, product, or service. There were virtually no negative feelings, however, when the conversational partner was aware of the agent's affiliation.

And the key conclusion:

Participation in an organized word-of-mouth marketing program does not undermine the effectiveness of word-of-mouth communication.

On the flip side, check out the reaction when people find out that a business paid someone to review or blog about a product and pretend they were unaffiliated:

In a 2007 study, 57 percent of people said they were less likely to buy a product if they suspected the company paid someone to write a positive review on an opinion site. Thirty percent of people say fake reviews or positive comments left by corporations are a big problem. That is compared to 20 percent in 2001. Clearly, people are becoming more skeptical and less tolerant about being misled. Since the above study shows the majority of people are not turned off by full disclosure, it is very clear that companies have a lot to lose and very little to gain by trying deceptive marketing techniques.

BLOGOLA

In the early days of radio, advertisers often quietly sent free products to the on-air talent hoping to get them to talk about the product on-air. Even worse, record companies would secretly pay in exchange for playing a song. Both of these practices were considered "payola," a form of bribery. In today's world, payola has given way to "blogola," sometimes called "blog groveling." The process involves companies enticing bloggers to generate buzz online by giving them free merchandise or other incentives to talk up a product while keeping their ties to the company under wraps. It is every bit as distasteful as payola was and even harder to hide, thanks to the ever-more-connected world in which we live. In addition to being caught more easily, those who engage in blogola stand to lose credibility and sales on a much wider scale.

Microsoft plugged its Acer Ferrari laptop by sending a fully outfitted computer preloaded with Windows Vista to about 90 bloggers to test. Many writers said they felt compelled to write positive things in exchange for the expensive equipment while other bloggers accused them of taking something that is tantamount to a bribe. In the letter that accompanied the computer, bloggers were given the option of returning the hardware to Microsoft, keeping it, or giving it away. After negative publicity about the event, Edelman, the PR firm that handled the promotion, then asked that the laptops be returned or given away when the bloggers were done with them so there would be no misinterpretation of the gesture. However, the damage had been done. Microsoft's image was tarnished and Edelman took a hit below the credibility belt too.

Sprint's credibility suffered a similar, although not as damaging, ding after it encouraged bloggers to try out its new Power Vision Network by sending them free phones and urging the writers to download music and movies at no cost. Many bloggers kept the device but some decided not to write about it, saying they had a strong aversion to writing about something just because a PR person wanted them to. Beyond the initial reaction to the idea of blogola, Sprint had a bigger problem on its hands: the product was lacking. Remember, the first rule of word-of-mouth marketing is to have a top-notch product or service to generate buzz. In the case of the Power Vision Network, the LG Fusic phone received some pretty harsh reviews ("really quite awful," wrote one blogger) and the service was panned for being overpriced. Not exactly the kind of buzz that Sprint was hoping for when it decided to send free phones to be reviewed.

AFTER-WORD

- Ethics are crucial to a good buzz campaign. The first time you give the public a reason to doubt you, your positive word of mouth tanks faster than the stock market after a sell-off.

- Before launching any campaign, visit the WOMMA (Word of Mouth Marketing Association) Web site and answer their 20-question ethics toolkit.

- The results of a deceptive word-of-mouth marketing effort can be disastrous, from failed products to boycotts. It is simply not worth the backlash to engage in false or misleading marketing.

- Being up front about an agent's affiliation with a brand does not translate into a lost sale. On the contrary, 75 percent of people were happy to continue their discussion with a brand ambassador as long as they felt the opinions they were getting were honest.

- On the other hand, 57 percent of the public said they were less likely to buy a product if they suspected the company was not being totally transparent in a word-of-mouth campaign.

- Blogola, or the practice of asking bloggers to give good feedback in exchange for free merchandise, is unethical. There is nothing wrong with seeding bloggers and letting them offer a fair review, but they should disclose the transaction as well as providing their honest opinion.

BAD WORDS

MANY businesses and marketers hesitate to use WOMM, fearing someone might say something bad about them. After all, if good word of mouth can travel at light speed, just how fast can bad WOM jettison across the Internet?

However, negative buzz can be managed and, in some cases, turned around to be more effective than good publicity would have been to begin with.

This chapter covers:

- Monitoring negative buzz

- Responding to negative buzz

- Turning a negative into a positive

- Promoting yourself

SOMETIMES BAD PRESS HAPPENS

You have worked hard to create a positive word-of-mouth campaign. You have dotted the "i," crossed the "t," and generally done your homework. Sometimes, negative buzz happens anyway.

You will not always be treated to good word of mouth. As Martha Stewart and Paris Hilton can attest to, rumors fly and people love to "diss" when given the chance. There are some who argue that any publicity — positive or negative — is good publicity because it keeps your name front and center. That is fairly easy to say as long as the word on the street is good; it is harder to remember when people are bashing you or your company. Just ask Michael Vick, United Way, or most members of the U.S. Congress. They would likely disagree that negative publicity is a good thing.

Moreover, nothing spreads faster than negative word of mouth — including positive buzz. Even when those great viral campaigns are tracking a million hits a week, negative campaigns could probably triple that. Whether people are griping about bad customer experiences hoping to get their revenge or a company is angling to get itself up higher on the hierarchy by fostering negative press about a competitor, bad buzz is going to spread, and quickly.

But wait, it gets worse. Not only will people jump on the bandwagon of bad publicity — they will likely make the reason sound much worse. After all, people like to embellish. They may not intentionally lie but they may try to make a bad story sound even worse by adding their own spin on it to make it sexier. It is a variation of the party game "telephone."

Say Margaret tells the story of a rude salesperson she encountered at the Jean Depot. Poor Margaret has been shopping for a new pair of jeans that will not make her behind look like the universe's biggest planet. She shares her tale of woe with Wilma, saying that the saleswoman chortled when Margaret asked if the jeans were available in a larger size. When Wilma tells her coworkers the story of Margaret's experience, she adds in a juicy detail about the saleswoman who now was smacking gum and talking on her cell phone while assisting Margaret. When Wilma's coworkers go to tell the story, the saleswoman was no longer a woman but a transvestite who verbally assaulted Margaret and tried to get her physically removed from the store. People often add details to make a story more entertaining, which hurts the company involved but amuses the audience. Even if they are telling the truth, the whole truth, and nothing but the truth without enhancement, if they are saying some not-so-nice things about you, you need to control it.

Bad press can cost you dearly. If someone is bad-mouthing you, current customers are likely to be turned off, or at least wary of doing business with you. Keep in mind the goal is to maintain a satisfied customer base first, and attract new clients second. If those who have already patronized your business are second-guessing themselves, it is a giant step in the wrong direction.

Then there are the prospective customers who were considering doing business with you but stop short when they hear nasty rumors. Or those who do not even know you exist until they hear something negative about your company. First impressions pack a powerful punch: There is virtually no way to turn that around.

Managing Negative Buzz

Now that you have read all the doom and gloom, there is some good news. You can contain negative buzz about your business — or at least manage it to keep it from spiraling so far out of control. Like most things, it requires common sense and a few rules.

WHAT ARE THEY SAYING?

First of all, pay attention to what people are saying about you. Many businesses rarely take the time to listen to the word on the street. It is far too easy to just assume everyone likes you and respects what your business is doing. That can prove to be a deadly mistake, especially when it is so simple to do some free research. Do a Google search of your name and your company's name. You can even set up a free Google Alert to let you know when something is being said online about your or your business.

However, Google may not tell the whole story. Investigate **Technorati.com** or **BlogPulse.com** to see how your reputation is faring. You can also check out Buzzmonitor software developed by the World Bank, which scans all RSS feeds. It can extract the source or root URL from the permalink, delete duplicates, and group all mentions in one place. It will not cost you a dime but can prove priceless when determining your online repute.

Ford Motor Company recently received some bad press after one of its fan clubs, the Black Mustang Club, tried to publish a calendar with pictures of members' cars. The word on the street was that Ford lawyers threatened to sue CafePress, the printer, if it printed the piece. Mustang owners and Ford fans at large were irate, to say the least. Some of the comments on online discussion boards included, "This is pathetic, Ford. Going after your own fan base is suicide" and "Are these companies out of their collective minds? Threatening to sue a fan club over the use of their logos and images of their cars. They must really hate making money."

Turns out it was all a misunderstanding that Ford was able to fix because the company paid attention to word on the street.

The automaker had simply asked the printer NOT to use any of Ford's logos or trademarks in a product to be sold, and that request was misconstrued to include all of Ford's products. Had the manufacturer not been paying attention, a breakdown in communication could have cost the company dearly. As it was, Ford managed to quell and correct the negative word of mouth relatively quickly.

RESPONDING TO BAD PRESS

With the advent of blogs, it is easier for people to share their negative experiences far and wide. You will have to develop a somewhat thicker skin if you want your company to survive, because it is likely that at some point you are going to read something about your business that is not-so-very nice. However, if you find several people are criticizing the same thing, take notice. Acknowledge their complaints. If you think what they are saying has merit, respond to their posts and say so. Tell that what you plan to do to fix the problem. Most importantly, thank them for their feedback. Show them that you listen, you care, and you are willing to respond. Most people will give you another chance if you admit you made a mistake and try to rectify it.

Now if you see something that strikes you as unfair, remember your manners. Yes, you still need to thank your customers for their feedback — even when it is something you did not want to hear. Respond to their comments by giving your side of the situation. Do not take the posts personally and do not ever engage in a debate with consumers. This is the time to remember the sage advice that the customer is always right. Be professional, be human, and be grateful you were able to respond in a public way to let others see how your company does business.

What you do not want to do is give your consumers a reason to bad-mouth you. That may sound like just good old Dr. Phil common sense, but you would be surprised at the companies that fall into that trap.

Take the phenomenon that is Harry Potter. In 2000, Warner Brothers sent letters to hundred of fan sites across the 'Net, claiming they had infringed on the company's property rights. They instructed the sites to shut down and even demanded the owners give Warner Brothers ownership of some of the domain names including HarryPotter-world.com. After a disgruntled teenaged fan went to the press, the story made headlines and two different activist organizations protested, organizing a boycott of all things Harry Potter. As you have already read, boycotts are a nasty business. So, before you go off on a power trip, ordering people around, be sure the trip is worthy of the ticket price; that is, is your position really so strong that it warrants losing both current and prospective customers over?

Hasbro and Mattel found themselves choosing their words carefully after they demanded that Facebook remove its Scrabulous application from the social networking site. The application was created by two brothers in Calcutta and boasted more than 500,000 daily players, which was roughly one quarter of the total people who had signed up for it.

Hasbro started yelling trademark infringement and threatened to shut it down. Clearly, there was some violation going on, but look at the powerful reach this decades-old game was enjoying. It re-ignited an interest in the game, with plenty of people going out and purchasing the board game after playing it online. However, the big, bad world of corporate lawyers decided the online version was too much of a threat to the good name of Scrabble. When the companies started discussing shutting it down, hundreds of people immediately launched a new Facebook group called "Save Scrabulous," leading to plenty of bad word of mouth for the manufacturers. The Hasbro and Mattel Web sites even posted links in the customer service areas so fans could protest. While they were content to hear the battle cry, the two game makers were more concerned about protecting the trademark than enjoying more visibility, loyalty, and sales. Can you spell I-G-N-O-R-A-M-U-S?

Target found itself in some proverbial hot blogosphere water when it refused to respond to a blogger who questioned one of its ads. The complainant wrote to the retailer about an ad showing a model lying spread-eagled atop the Target logo, with the center of the target appearing at the crux of the woman's spread legs. It should not have mattered whether the comment came from a blogger or a school teacher; Target should have taken the opportunity to acknowledge the writer's concerns. Instead it responded with the following reply:

> Thank you for contacting Target; unfortunately we are unable to respond to your inquiry because Target does not participate with non-traditional media outlets. This practice is in place to allow us to focus on publications that reach our core guest.
>
> Once again, thank you for your interest and have a nice day.

The retailer managed to bungle that one on a couple of different levels. Mistake number one: Target just implied that nontraditional media (bloggers) are not core guests of store. My guess is that many of them were not after that statement. Mistake number two: Target insulted a huge, and ever-growing, media source. A 2007 study by Synovate/Marketing Daily shows that 78 percent of people aged 18 to 24 have visited a blog, as have 45 percent of older Americans, and roughly 20 percent of people who read blogs follow them daily. That means plenty of opportunity for Target to generate bad publicity with this move and plenty of people were exposed to that negative buzz.

PROMOTE YOURSELF

This is a tactic you should be using anyway but it is imperative to control negative buzz. Get your business promoted on the first page of a search. Many people will only scan the first references they find to a search so cater to them. Be sure the correct and positive information about your company is front and center. At the very least, be sure that **Wikipedia.com** has a true and accurate listing for your business because it shows up very high in search rankings so it is an ideal place to correct misinformation or quell rumors.

Southwest Airlines found itself wishing it could fly under the radar after a customer service supervisor told a young female passenger that she was dressed too provocatively to fly. An employee of the Dallas-based airline asked a 23-year-old to change her outfit from a frayed miniskirt. The story made headlines as consumers pointed out the company's early prominent ad campaigns in 1971 featuring hot-pants-clad flight attendants. Shortly thereafter, CEO Gary Kelly offered a public apology, even recording ads for national radio describing lower fares to match the miniskirt.

Southwest took a potentially devastating public relations move and owned up to its mistake, even daring to poke fun at itself by having lower fares that match higher hemlines. The public is far more forgiving of a company that can admit a mistake. As

Ben McConnell, author of Citizen Marketers, said, "Being true to a culture that has paved your way to success — and continues to sustain it — is always the better decision in the long run of reputation management."

Turn a Negative Into a Positive

Dell Computer has faced a slew of negative publicity for something as innocuous as a "boring" corporate blog to poor customer service. The final blow came after a Dell laptop exploded and caught fire during a conference in Japan (no one was hurt). As you can imagine, negative buzz abounded.

Dell listened to the criticism, as painful as it was. The company launched its new IdeaStorm Web site as a self-described "new way to listen to customers on how to build the best products and services." Essentially, they created an online community where people could post their ideas and discuss them with other users as well as with Dell employees. Users could tell the company exactly what was unsatisfactory about customer service, knowing that the executives were listening to them. Dell also created the Direct2Dell blog so that the company could have a more targeted and candid conversation with its users.

As a result, many critics changed their tune. Dell proved that it cares about what the customer thinks. The company addressed its negatives head-on, listening to what needed to be done and acknowledging where it could make improvements. It did not engage in debate with the nay-sayers; it simply tried to do things better, and it worked. It created good word of mouth by getting detractors to change their minds and admit the company had turned things around. When a negative review can do so much more damage than a positive review, it is easy to see why turning a critic into a fan is a powerful way to spin word of mouth in right direction.

Other companies are hoping to have the same success. Pet owners were deeply concerned in 2007 when Menu Foods, a national manufacturer of pet foods, issued a recall after some of its canned and pouched foods caused thousands of cats and dogs to become ill or die. Fluffy and Fido's owners were not the only ones affected, however. The recall produced a ripple effect that impacted sales at national pet stores.

In the wake of the recall, both PetSmart and PETCO wisely issued an email to their customers to recap the situation and reassure customers. Smart: they took a proactive approach, and they reached out to their consumers. But only one of them used the opportunity to really connect with its core audience. Compare the two examples:

PETCO EMAIL TO CUSTOMERS

Dear [customer's first name],

PETCO cares about your pet. Here at PETCO the health and well being of your pet is our number one priority and we'd like to update you about the recent industry recall of certain WET DOG AND CAT FOOD PRODUCTS.

First, it is important that you know ALL foods affected by the recent Menu Foods recall have been pulled from our stores' shelves and are not being sold online at PETCO.com. For additional information regarding the recalled pet food brands, you can visit the Menu Foods Web site [embedded link].

Second, where possible, we are sending notices to anyone who may have purchased recalled products asking that they discontinue feeding their dog or cat these specific canned and pouched wet foods.

Sincerely,

Jim Myers, CEO

PETCO turned a bad situation into a decent PR opportunity, warmly engaging their customer by name, with a signature from the CEO making the message a little more personal. The company also reassured owners with the first line "PETCO cares about your pet." Contrast that to the email issued by PetSmart:

PETSMART EMAIL TO CUSTOMERS

Dear Valued PetSmart customer:

As you probably have heard, Menu Foods, a national manufacturer of pet foods, issued a voluntary recall of canned and pouched wet dog and cat food manufactured in two of its facilities between December 2006 and March 2007. Again, this is a recall of a specific type of wet pet food made by Menu Foods. Other wet pet foods and all dry pet foods and treats are not impacted by this recall.

Menu Foods initiated the recall after receiving reports that some of its foods may be the cause of reported illnesses and kidney failure in dogs and cats. Menu Foods distributes these products to supermarkets, mass merchandisers, and pet-specialty stores, including PetSmart, under a variety of brand names.

Sincerely,

Philip L. Frances

Chairman & CEO, PetSmart, Inc.

Unlike the recalled food, PetSmart's letter is coarse and dry with little emotion. It sounds as though it were crafted very carefully to say the right thing legally, but without concern for the fears pet owners were feeling. The company missed a strong opportunity to connect with and reassure pet owners that it cared about the health and well being of their animals.

As for the manufacturer at the center of all of this, Menu Foods, the fallout from this recall is massive. The manufacturer faces several lawsuits, and it remains to be seen whether the company can weather the storm of public outcry.

The entire episode is a lesson in public relations 101, but it is a prime example of the need to effectively manage negative word of mouth. By proactively responding to the bad buzz and by making its customers feel that they, and their pets, were of utmost importance, PETCO managed to take a publicity nightmare and turn it into an opportunity for positive customer relations. And that seems as good a place as any to paws this discussion on word-of-mouth marketing — for now.

AFTER-WORD

- Nothing spreads more quickly than negative word of mouth. Not only will it travel faster than the speed of light but it is likely to be exaggerated in its journey, making the fallout that much worse.

- Keep bad press in check by knowing what people are saying about you. Monitor the Web and know what is being written online about your business. Keep an eye on what is being said about your industry, too — if the whole industry is getting a bad rep, you need to know it so your business can distance itself from the negativity.

- If you get even a whiff of bad buzz, respond quickly, clearly, and on message. Thank the consumers for their feedback. Acknowledge complaints with respect.

- If you feel that negative publicity is unwarranted, offer your side of the story but do not engage in debate. Stick to the facts and be courteous to your complainants.

- Do not just respond to any bad press; market yourself in a positive way (both before and during a crisis of reputation).

- The best defense to negative publicity is not to need one. Do not give people a reason to bad-mouth you. Stay focused on the great product you have to offer, market it in a way that is ethical and attention getting, and let your satisfied customers build you some fantastic word of mouth.

Conclusion: Famous Last Words

Most people agree that word of mouth is infinitely powerful. I cannot tell you how many small business owners I spoke with while writing this book who gushed, "Word of mouth is everything. My whole business was built on it!" When I asked them what they had done to perpetuate it, most had no answer. They were fully aware of its clout but totally clueless when it came to harnessing it.

That is likely because for decades, word of mouth has just occurred naturally. Consumers talked; they shared opinions. There was no need to define it or examine it. Word of mouth just happened.

So what has changed? Plenty. Your customer has so many more ways to communicate. People talk, they text, and they Twitter. Sometimes, they do all three at once.

Marketing has to change too. Once you acknowledge that, you can put word of mouth to work as an extraordinary tool. Only then will you understand that you did not really have a choice. People will only grow warier of traditional marketing, becoming even more reliant on the opinions of a trusted source. You must engage consumers on a more personal level. When you can create in them a sense of loyalty, the feeling that they have some connection to your brand, you have the essence of word-of-mouth marketing in the palm of your hand.

That is when you will know you have fully embraced word of mouth. Then you just need to set it free and let it work its magic.

Appendix A: Proven Secrets & Tips for WOMM

Use your distribution channels wisely. Anyone from sales representatives to wholesalers and consultants to industry experts is an influential person to help you further word of mouth. Make the most of that influence! Tell them about your product or service. Give them information they can share with others. Share with them the stories of your successful clients. It all adds up to nurturing natural mouthpieces for your buzz.

Consider Krispy Kreme doughnuts, which landed on the map back in 1937 with its light-as-a-feather treat. The original owner planned to sell his baked goods in grocery stores but when customers got a whiff of the über-food, they clamored for more. The owner simply cut a hole in the bakery wall to serve patrons who could not get enough hot, fresh doughnuts. Not a traditional distribution channel, to be sure, but an effective one.

Tie a buzz campaign into an event. The event does not have to be a national holiday, although it certainly can be. It just needs to be something that underscores your message, your niche, or your name. For instance, Bison Brewing Company in Berkeley, California, produces the only commercially brewed sparkling alcoholic beverage in the country that combines whole tea leaves and a few exotic ingredients. The owner leveraged the 229th anniversary of the Boston Tea Party to host his own "tea party." Anyone who came in with a plain tea bag got a free pint of his Bison Original Hard Iced Tea in exchange. I have never engaged in reading tea leaves but I have to believe that his business's future looked brighter after that little move.

Cater to your champions. These are your brand evangelists. Educate them about new products or services you are offering. Engage them in the design process if possible, so they have an even greater vested interest in seeing your company succeed. You can reach them and teach them via seminars, newsletters, Web sites, or any other vehicle. The approach will not matter — the effort will.

Get people's attention. There is no question it is easier to hawk a new, state-of-the-art, tech-y gadget than it is to get people jazzed about something more mundane like a razor or a nail clipper. But no matter how run-of-the-mill your product may seem, there are still ways to get people talking about it. Charmin brand toilet paper did just that when it built the 20-stall Potty Palooza in the heart of New York's Times Square during the height of the holiday shopping season. Procter & Gamble operated a spiffed-up public restroom, amply stocked with Charmin Ultra, uniformed attendants, and a six-foot stuffed bear for photo ops (after visitors left the stalls, of course). If Charmin can get people talking about toilet paper, I cannot think of much that would not be buzz-worthy. I guess this stunt could have been called word-of-potty-mouth marketing but it worked, with great visibility.

Even good old-fashioned duct tape can be marketable. Henkel Consumer Adhesives, a manufacturer of duct tape, hosts a "Stuck at Prom" contest, where attendees festoon themselves in tuxedos and gowns made of the sticky stuff. Among the reasons listed on the company's Web site for donning a taped outfit: resistant to spills, quick weight loss with the product's sauna-like nature, and easy rip patching.

Leverage traditional media. Word of mouth works, but it works even better when it is used in conjunction with more traditional forms of media. According to Brad Fay of the Keller Fay Group, nearly 40 percent of word-of-mouth recommendations occur in conversations that start with a reference to a newspaper article, television or radio show, or advertising. As a result, you will not be able to ignore the usual channels of communication. Piggyback on them. Use word of mouth as one form of marketing but support it through more traditional means to get the most for your money.

Good customer service is crucial. I cannot stress this enough. When you evaluate how well you are serving your clients, consider things like efficiency, consistency, convenience, reliability, accessibility, and responsiveness. Find out which of these are most important to your target customers and then find out how well you score. Create your own report card and take a good, hard look at the grades you give yourself. If you find room for improvement, fill it.

Respond, respond, and then respond faster. And better. Nothing is more disheartening than a customer who lodges a complaint and either a) gets no response, or b) hears something so long after the infraction that he or she forgot they griped in the first place. Ignoring complaints is a proven method of getting people to talk about you — but not in the way you want.

Appendix B: More Types of Low-Cost (or Free!) WOMM Campaigns

You have just spent untold hours reading all the secrets to word-of-mouth marketing and now you want more? Good. You got it. There are a few other ways to generate buzz that do not fall into the categories in the book so I am including them here. Think of it as your prize for reading all the way to the end (without consuming all the carbohydrates and calories in a box of Cracker Jacks).

Endorsement Marketing

You have already read how powerful testimonials can be. When someone you trust recommends something, you are more likely to listen. What if I told you that you could nudge that recommendation along to help you land more clients? Interested? Read on.

Endorsement marketing takes testimonials and uses them to the power of 10. Funnily enough, there are ten steps to a successful endorsement campaign. What is different about this campaign? You start it on your own behalf, you carry it through each of the steps, and you wind up with more buzz and prospective clients than Imelda Marcos has shoes — but it is all based on someone else's recommendation.

Basically it boils down to you tooting your own horn. You will write a glowing recommendation for yourself that will appear to come from your client (with the client's approval). You will create a list of prospects along with contact information. The client will provide letterhead and envelopes (which is the only expense required of your client). You will mail your letters out and do the necessary follow-up.

That, in a nutshell, is endorsement marketing. The specific steps, provided by Nancy Michaels (whose case study can be found just after this), follow. Think of it as a pitch letter that is far more effective.

Step One — Get Over Yourself

No, I do not mean you are too big for your britches. I mean you need to get over your fears. It is hard to ask someone to endorse you, even though you know you have delivered a great product or service. Get over that fear. Most clients would love to help you if they knew how. Here is your chance to let them.

Tell them how fortunate you feel to have served them in some capacity (you should have already done this many times over anyway) and ask if they would be willing to help you grow your business.

Step Two — Make a Specific Request

You will be doing the work here, not your client. Be sure the client knows that this requires little effort on his or her part. Spell out to them the foundation of the campaign as described above. You will be writing the endorsement letter, you will create a target list, and you will handle addressing and mailing the letter to your prospects. The only thing you are asking of your client is to read and (hopefully) agree to what you write, and to provide letterhead and envelopes.

Step Three — Return the Favor

As you are pitching your client, be sure they know you are more than willing to return the favor in some way. Whether they need you to work on one of their projects as barter, or represent them in some way — they get to name what their favor is. You should commit to a dollar amount in advance, though; offer to work off a $1,000 fee, or whatever you deem reasonable for the favor they are doing you. Be sure this is settled up front so there are no hard feelings down the road.

Step Four — Identify Your Prospects

Who do you want to target? Who needs to know about your business? Who is likely to help generate some buzz within your industry? These are the people to include on your prospect list.

TIP: *If there is a magazine targeted at your market, take a look at who is advertising in it. Those would be ideal companies to include.*

Step Five — Draft Your Endorsement Letter

This is no time for modesty. Write about your company as though you are the client. Pen everything you hope your client would say about you. Use bullet points. Highlight the results you have achieved for that client. Keep the letter short and to the point, factual, and focused.

Step Six — All Systems Go

Offer your client the opportunity to review your draft. Keep in mind these are your words but they are supposedly coming from your client's brain — they should have a chance to read and agree with what you have written. Once you have agreed on a final draft, scan the client's signature on to your letter and let the United States Postal Service work its magic.

TIP: *If you are a sole proprietor or do not have administrative help, consider hiring a virtual assistant to help you with the mailing. This process can be administratively intense.*

Step Seven — Draft Your Next Letter

Within two weeks of sending out your first letter, prepare a follow-up letter to go to the same list of prospects (unless you have heard back from them after the first letter. In that case, congratulations!). This letter will come from you, not the client. Include testimonials from other clients or articles you have written. This second letter helps keep you top in their mind, as well as generate more interest in and awareness of your company.

Step Eight — Finesse Your Follow-Up

Be prepared to receive responses from your letters. That means you will need to be ready to make phone calls, schedule face-to-face meetings, send out additional information, and anything else that may require your attention as a result of your prospecting.

TIP: *Keep a detailed list of who contacts you from each business, as your letter may have been forwarded to a more appropriate person within the company.*

Step Nine — Draft and Send a Final Letter

Two weeks after your second letter, you should send another one. Keep it clear, concise, and captivating. Include a sample case study of how your company helped a client. Provide additional references who can attest to your business's value. It is also a good idea to make a copy of the original letter that your client sent out, and include it in this mailing. Sound like overkill? It is not. It is smart marketing and taking advantage of the fact that your company's name is still freshly rattling around inside your prospect's brain.

Step Ten — Calling All Contacts

It is time to get on the phone with anyone who has not yet responded to your campaign. Find out where your letters ended up — they may have simply gone to the wrong person. Experts recommend that you send your endorsement letters and ensuing correspondence to no more than 100 people so that you can adequately do the follow-up work necessary to make each of these contacts achievable and meaningful.

TIP: *Take note of all the names you receive throughout this process; use them to create and maintain a marketing communications plan to keep in touch with each of the people you have touched base with.*

CASE STUDY: NANCY MICHAELS

Grow Your Business, Inc.

60 Thoreau Street, #308

Concord, MA 01742

www.growyourbusinessnetwork.com

781-860-8818 phone

617-905-4711 cell

Nancy Michaels - President

Author, speaker, consultant, small business owner

I heard about endorsement marketing at a seminar and found it to be a very effective way to achieve instant credibility that would ultimately lead to great word-of-mouth marketing. More importantly, I knew it could inspire inbound calls to my office as opposed to cold calling to get my foot in the door.

CASE STUDY: NANCY MICHAELS

It was crucial to me that I had a great relationship with a trusted client who was willing to endorse my work. I had a two-year relationship and a stellar track record with my corporate client before I would ask them to do this for me. I also took all of the leg work away from them and, with the exception of asking for their corporate letterhead and mailing envelopes, I took care of the administrative efforts associated with the campaign.

My endorsement marketing campaign distinguished me from my competitors because I had a fabulous reference from a major corporation who was my client. That separated me from other potential suppliers to these companies. And as a result of the campaign, I've enjoying an enhanced reputation among prospects, more face-to-face and phone meetings, and two signed corporate contracts. It's been so successful that I'm working on a 75-company campaign as we speak.

When my phone began ringing, I knew I was on to something and it made it much easier for me to pick up the phone and follow up with the corporations I hadn't yet heard from.

Referral Marketing

Many people realize that referrals, organic word of mouth, are critical to any business's existence. After all, you have just read an entire book on the subject. There must be something to it, right? The catch is that few people understand how to harness the power of referrals. It is actually pretty simple to do.

You start by building a circle, which becomes your network. Identify the people in your area who are likely to be good sources for referrals. Create a list of 10 careers whose members are most often in touch with just the kind of customer you want to target. If you own a title company, this may include real estate agents, mortgage brokers, lawyers, bankers, movers, furniture retailers, and the like. A wedding photographer should write down occupations including jewelers, bridal consultants, bakers, DJs, musicians, and florists. These are people who will deal every day with just the kinds of customers you need.

Now, actively find 10 people working in each career field. Call them, visit their shops, or introduce yourself at industry trade shows. Make an appointment to meet with them to discuss your business and theirs. Tell them about your business, your specialty, and what differentiates you from your competition. Ask them to keep you in mind when they meet someone who needs the service or product you provide. Referrals go both ways, so let them know you can generate business for them at the same time they are helping you.

Once you have found 10 people in 10 careers, you have a circle of 100 people networking on your behalf. And unlike traditional networking groups, where many members do not often interact with members of your target customers, these are people who come into contact with them every day.

Do not be afraid to ask friends or family for introductions to people they know in your target occupations. Most people either have or know an accountant, an attorney, a real estate agent, and others who will be an excellent source of referrals for you. As long as the introductions are made with the understanding that you will be helping them grow their business as well, there are precious few small business owners who would turn down the opportunity to at least meet with you. If you find someone who balks, just move on. There are plenty of other people doing that job and you only need to find 10 of them.

After you have your circle of 100 referral partners, keep in touch with them. You do not have to email them weekly or send them flowers for their birthdays, but you want to be sure you still come to mind when they meet a potential customer four months from now. In a busy world, it is easy to forget. Check in with each partner every so often so you will be fresh in their mind the next time an opportunity arises to send business your way.

Do not be discouraged if you find that some people never seem to send any business your way. After all, that is part of the reason you developed so many referral partners to begin with. If you find that your relationship has not been beneficial, you can always find another professional in the same occupation and strike up a partnership with them. Chances are, the rest of your network will keep you busy enough that you might not even notice for a while, which means word of mouth is working its magic.

Article Marketing

Writing articles is a powerful and easy way to attract your target market to your Web site and get people talking about you and your business. It helps to establish you as an expert, and can help with lead generation, increased Web site traffic, and even improved search engine rank, all of which helps build buzz. The cherry on the top is that it costs very little, if any, money. It just takes some time, some knowledge, and some smart marketing.

Do not concern yourself if you are small business owner feeling lost in a sea of bigger fish. Part of the beauty of article marketing is that it promotes your credibility. You can earn the trust of readers who learn from you and realize you are a good source of information. If you provide good information, you must know what you are talking about, right? Right! So this is a prime way for you to take on the big boys in your industry and win.

If you write pieces that are helpful and well written, they are likely to be snatched up by other Web sites and linked to by bloggers. Be specific and avoid hype. At the same time, you need to write the kind of article that will capture attention. "How-to" articles are prime examples of pieces that are readily republished by others.

Try writing interesting articles that are related to your Web site, your product, or your industry. They should be original, with quality content. The best articles are focused, easy to read, and informative. They are also the most likely to be picked up for distribution. These are not sales missives; they are similar to e-newsletters in that they are editorial in content with perhaps a slight promotional aspect.

It should go without saying, but I will say it anyway: A strong headline is critical to successful article marketing. It needs to include strong keywords and be interesting enough to click on. Otherwise, the world may never know how much you have to contribute to the subject.

Articles can include links for readers to glean more information; however, be wary. Do not include too many links. Do not make the majority of links point to your Web site (remember: slight promotional aspect).

Distribute them to article directories and submission sites. Examples include sites like Ezine Articles (**ezinearticles.com**) and **articlemarketer.com**. This is not the time to be territorial; you should offer permission for others to republish your work on their blog, Web site, or in their email newsletter. After all, the more people who publish you, the farther word of mouth spreads.

Another no-brainer: Post your article on your Web site. I know you already knew that but I had to say it anyway. It is the Virgo in me.

Resource Box

If you want your article to bring readers to your Web site, you need to write the perfect resource box. This is the bio that appears at the end of your article. (If you want to feel like you are in the know, call it a SIG — short for signature. Sure to impress!) It should include your name and title, your Web site, your brief message, and perhaps a call to action. Your hope is that readers will click on your URL in the resource box and be mesmerized by your Web site.

You will be able to track incoming links from Web sites as well as the number of times the article was reprinted in non-Web site publications. Article marketing is another viral-type marketing that offers the allure of high visibility and strong return on investment for very little money.

Search Engine Optimization

Otherwise known as SEO (as opposed to a CEO, to which we could all aspire), search engine optimization deals with Web page order when readers are searching by key words or phrases. In other words, it is sort of like making your business popular — the higher a page is ranked, the more traffic it is likely to get. Since more traffic typically means more sales, you can see why plenty of people care more about their SEO than most CEOs.

I know you are asking, "What does SEO have to do with article marketing, and in turn, with creating word of mouth?" The answer is everything. Say that your Web site has more links to it than your competitor's. It will be seen higher in search engines, which means more people will likely check out your site before your nemesis. You have already read that in your carefully crafted resource box, you will include a link to your Web site. If you use article marketing to get your well-written piece printed in multiple locations, that is a lot of linking going on. The more articles you get posted, the more links are out there, and the more traffic is making a beeline for your site. Sit back and get ready to be buzzed.

OTHER POSSIBILITIES

Once you have perfected the art (and science) of generating word of mouth online, you should remember local opportunities to spread some buzz offline. Here are a few other tried-and-true methods of getting your business name noticed. Remember, people need to know you exist before they can talk about you. Try some of these tools, offer an outstanding product and unbeatable customer service, and you are on your way to sporting more word of mouth than Elizabeth Taylor has spouses.

- Post flyers on bulletin boards in grocery stores, coffee shops, churches, libraries, hair salons, and community centers.

- Position your business as a community resource by sending well-written letters to the editor of your local newspaper.

- Submit event information to free community calendar listings on local broadcast stations and in area papers.

- Ask current clients or supporters to pass out extra materials as they go about their daily business. Offer an incentive of some sort to make this even more successful.

- Participate in local groups, such as Rotary, Lions, or Kiwanis clubs where networking occurs naturally.

ABOUT THE AUTHOR

Lynn Thorne

Photo by Penny McGoey

Lynn Thorne is the creative force behind Lollipop Copy, a communications firm with clients that include JCPenney Direct, *The Washington Post*, USNews Ventures, and CTIA. Previously, she was the editorial director of America's Promise — The Alliance for Youth as well as a news anchor/reporter for television stations in Richmond, Virginia; Wausau, Wisconsin; and Charlottesville, Virginia. She resides in Maryland with her husband and two young sons.

Glossary

Action: What participants do to create, pass along, or respond to a WOMUnit

Affiliate Marketing: Online partnerships between advertisers and publishers

Amplified Word of Mouth: Marketer-enhanced word-of-mouth campaign in which professionals encourage WOM between consumers

Blog: Short for "Weblog," an online journal linking to other sites and news stories

Blogger: A person who writes a blog

Blogola: Money or products secretly given to bloggers in exchange for positive reviews

Blogvertorial: Advertising or paid content posted on a blog

Buzz: Excitement or animated discussion about a brand, product, or service

Buzz Marketing: A viral marketing technique to get people talking about a product or service

CAN-SPAM Act: Legislation passed in 2003 that limits what unsolicited email can be sent

Cause Marketing: The partnership between a nonprofit and a for-profit on behalf of a cause

Clarity: Whether the message is understood by the receiver of a WOMUnit

Community Marketing: Marketing to any group of people with common interests, including user groups, fan clubs, and discussion forums

Consumptions: The receiver directly consumes the WOMUnit but takes no further action

Content Sharing: The free distribution of useful company knowledge to inspire WOM

Conversions: The receiver completes a desired action after consuming the WOMUnit

Customer Generated Media (CGM): Any kind of content created by the consumer instead of the marketer

Depth: The aspects and/or qualities that increase the persuasiveness of a WOMUnit

Discussion Forum/Board: User-generated content online

Doglish: Slang or jargon that is easily misunderstood by the receiver

Drawbridge: What it takes for word of mouth to jump across a weak tie

Eighty/Twenty Rule: A commonly held belief that 80 percent of a company's business comes from 20 percent of its customers

Evangelist: Passionate consumers who influence their friends on behalf of a company

Event Marketing: Face-to-face promotional experiences between customers and companies

E-zine: Electronic magazines and/or newsletters

Faux Blog: A fake blog created by a company or person to generate good WOM

Focus Group: A research group conducted with a small number of consumers to discuss or evaluate new products

Flog: See Faux Blog

Geotargeting: Method of determining the geographical location of a Web site visitor and delivering customized content based on their location

Guerilla Marketing: Undercover marketing techniques in which full disclosure does not occur

Honesty ROI: WOM that is based on the honesty of relationship, opinion, and identity

Influencer Marketing: The practice of identifying key decision makers in a target audience and encouraging them to use their influence to spread WOM

Influentials: Key decision makers within a target audience

Inquiries: The receiver seeks more information after consuming the WOMUnit

Keywords: Words or phrases that people use to find products and services online

Landing Page: The page that appears online when a reader clicks on an ad or search engine result link

Loyalty Program: Structured marketing efforts that reward buying behavior

Microsharing: See Content Sharing

Microsite (also know as minisite): A separately promoted page of a Web site with its own URL

Moral Hazard: The differences in how people will behave based on whether they are affected by a WOMUnit

Organic Word-of-Mouth: Naturally occurring word of mouth between people who are discussing a product or service

Participants: The individuals whose actions make up a WOM episode — may be the creator, the sender, the receiver, or a combination of the above

Peer-to-Peer Marketing: The transparent spread of WOM from person to person

Performer-to-Peer Marketing: The undercover marketing effort of a company trying to generate WOM

Podcast: A collection of digital media files distributed over the Internet for playback on computers or audio players

Polarity: Whether the message content received by a participant is positive or negative

Re-creations: The receiver creates a new WOMUnit after

consuming a WOMUnit

Referral Program: A marketing program that rewards customers for bringing in new prospects

Relays: When a receiver redistributes the WOMUnit

RSS (Rich Site Summary): A format for delivering and regularly changing Web content

Seeding: The practice of marketers giving away products to influencers in the hopes that they will spread WOM

SEO (Search Engine Optimization): Driving as much traffic as possible to a Web site based on using key words and search terms

Shill Marketing: See Guerilla Marketing

Social Networking: An online place where a user can create a profile and build a personal network that connects him or her to other users

Stealth Marketing: See Guerilla Marketing

Technorati: A blog search engine

Timeliness: Whether the WOMUnit arrives in time to be relevant to a campaign

Topicality: The degree that the marketing message is contained in the WOMUnit

Undercover Marketing: See Guerilla Marketing

URL (Uniform Resource Locator): The address of a file accessible on the Internet

Venue: The medium or physical location where a communication takes place

Viral Marketing: Entertaining or informative messages that are meant to be forwarded from person to person, usually electronically

Weak Ties: Clusters of people who are not strongly linked

Widget: A portable snippet of code that can be installed on a Web page to provide visitors with information, games, or functionality

Wiki: A piece of server software that allows users to freely create and edit Web page content

Word of Mouth (WOM): The act of consumers talking among themselves about a product or service

Word-of-Mouth Marketing (WOMM): An effort by marketers or businesses to encourage word of mouth among consumers

WOMMA (Word of Mouth Marketing Association): The nonprofit trade association for the word-of-mouth industry

WOMUnit: A single unit of marketing-relevant information shared by a consumer

INDEX

A

Advertising 14-16, 26, 30-32, 39, 43, 46-48, 51, 59, 80, 85, 86, 89, 119, 123, 125, 141, 142, 150, 152, 155, 162, 172-174, 180, 181, 186, 190, 191, 194, 257, 52

Amplified 20, 27, 41, 47

B

Benefits 22, 42, 43, 48, 64, 78, 111, 123, 147, 193, 200, 202, 206, 212, 220

Billboard 153, 154

Blog 22, 36, 38, 41, 71, 74, 75, 104, 117, 122, 131, 145, 162-173, 175, 174, 195, 196, 206, 207, 231, 234, 235, 246, 247, 268, 275, 277, 279

Book 20, 24, 26, 33, 52, 54, 62, 95, 100, 113, 143-145, 199, 204, 224, 225, 231, 253, 259, 265

Buzz 20, 28, 34-37, 41-43, 45-48, 58, 59, 74, 75, 80, 81, 83-85, 90, 92-95, 97, 98, 101, 103-107, 109, 111, 112, 115, 118, 119, 121, 123, 124, 127, 128, 130-133, 137, 140-143, 145, 146, 149, 155, 156, 158, 164, 168, 170, 188, 194, 197, 198, 208, 209, 214-216, 218, 220, 221, 224, 229, 235, 236, 239-241, 246, 247, 250, 255-257, 259-261, 267, 270

C

Cause Marketing 194, 221

Commercial 28, 35, 40, 65, 30, 91, 95, 130, 161, 163, 178

Communicate 195, 253

Computer 26, 66, 67, 97, 140, 204, 235

Consumer 111, 118, 153, 211, 220, 226, 232, 276, 280

D

Demand 31, 80, 146

Design 71, 152, 172, 187, 256

E

Email Marketing 30, 177-182, 186, 189-191, 208, 220

Endorsement 14, 25, 69, 211, 260, 261, 264, 265

Ethics 20, 46, 94, 174, 223, 224, 228, 236

F

Free 26, 27, 29, 37, 43, 48, 60, 62, 63, 67, 72-74, 85, 86, 89-93, 95, 103, 119, 132-135, 137, 141-144, 146, 151, 159, 162, 165, 171, 174, 187, 200, 204, 206, 207, 209, 212, 226, 235-237, 242, 254, 256, 270, 276

Fundamentals 30

G

Guarantee 185, 228

I

Influence 22-24, 28, 38, 203, 255, 277

Internet 37, 41, 44, 45, 63, 90, 109-112, 115, 119, 124, 149, 165, 169, 174, 178, 182, 194, 200, 202, 206, 217, 239, 278, 279

L

Language 26

M

Magazine 14, 31, 35, 143, 208, 213, 262

Marketing 15, 16, 19-36, 41, 37, 42-52, 55, 59, 60, 61, 66, 67, 70-74, 77, 81, 83-95, 98, 99, 101-103, 105, 106, 109-112, 114, 117, 118, 121, 123, 124, 127-131, 133, 134, 136, 140, 141, 143-145, 147-149, 151-154, 156-159, 161-163, 170, 172, 174, 177-182, 186, 189-191, 193, 194, 199, 204, 205, 208, 209, 211-213, 216, 217, 220, 221, 223, 224, 226, 232-234, 236, 250, 254, 257, 259, 260, 263-265, 267-270, 275, 277-280

Messaging 16, 22, 41, 127, 133, 147, 148, 154, 158

Money 24, 25, 27, 32-34, 42, 43, 51, 53, 54, 59, 67, 72, 79, 80, 88-90, 96, 97, 123, 125, 143, 144, 148, 150, 151, 167, 179, 197, 198, 200, 202, 204, 206, 211, 216, 224, 242, 257, 267, 269

N

Newspaper 14, 31, 99, 166, 195, 257, 270

O

Opportunities 40, 44, 82, 100, 195, 213, 215, 270

Organic 20, 27, 41, 47, 163, 209, 265

Original 35, 63, 118, 199, 255, 263, 268

P

Performer-To-Peer 92, 94, 95, 124

Phone 52, 58, 76, 94, 99, 100, 111, 116, 133, 138-141, 169, 213, 177, 196, 212, 264, 241, 263, 264

Photos 35, 70, 123, 156, 157

Podcasting 194, 205, 220

Print 14, 100, 121, 19, 233

Product 25, 28, 29, 30, 45, 58,61, 68, 77, 79, 200, 205, 206, 210, 211, 213, 220, 220, 224, 225, 232, 227, 231-237, 243, 251, 255-257, 266-268, 270, 275

Promote 194, 196, 199, 211, 212

Public 85, 86, 198, 210, 214, 215, 217, 220, 223, 226-229, 236, 237, 243, 246, 250, 256

R

Reputation 50, 57, 169, 194, 215-217, 221, 232, 242, 247, 251, 265

S

Service 14-16, 22, 23, 27, 30, 32-34, 37, 39, 44-46, 49, 51-54, 57, 58, 60, 65-68, 78, 80, 81, 84, 86, 91, 108, 93, 107, 110, 113, 116, 120-122, 125, 130, 131, 135, 132, 143, 144, 146, 148, 162, 172, 178, 190, 212, 217, 224, 225, 228, 230, 234, 236, 245-247, 255, 257, 260, 266, 270, 275

Social Networking 36, 66, 115, 199, 200, 202, 203, 205, 220, 229, 244

Survey 22, 38, 75, 86, 107, 132,
    148, 157, 162, 178, 224,
    225

T

Telemarketing 30
Television 30, 257, 273
Testimonials 16, 216
Tracking 28, 48, 79, 89, 101,
    103, 105, 116, 127, 145,
    197, 240

V

Viral 20, 41, 45, 46, 86, 103,
    147-151, 152-154, 155-159,
    193, 194, 199, 220, 240,
    269, 275

W

Web 24, 28, 30, 35, 36, 51,
    61, 62, 66-68, 77, 78, 80,
    90, 92, 94, 100, 102-104,
    110-115, 121, 123, 124,
    132, 135, 136, 139, 140,
    147, 151-157, 159, 165,
    168, 170, 173, 179, 182,
    186, 187, 189, 190, 196,
    199, 201, 203, 204, 207,
    214, 217, 227, 229, 233,
    236, 245, 247, 248, 250,
    256, 257, 267-270, 277-280
Word-of-mouth 19, 20, 23, 24,
    27, 26, 30, 34, 37-39, 43-50,
    52, 55, 65, 66, 72-74, 81,
    83, 91, 94, 95, 97, 101, 105,
    106, 107, 113, 118, 124,
    125, 127-131, 133, 134,
    136, 140, 145, 148, 157,
    158, 162, 163, 193, 194,
    204, 208, 209, 214, 216,
    217, 220, 221, 223, 224,
    232-234, 236, 237, 239,
    250, 254, 257, 259, 264,
    275, 280
Words 20, 31, 33, 82, 103-106,
    114, 119, 125, 127, 140,
    148, 166, 172, 182, 195,
    214, 218, 230, 244, 262,
    269, 279

ONLINE MARKETING SUCCESS STORIES:

INSIDER SECRETS FROM THE EXPERTS WHO ARE MAKING MILLIONS ON THE INTERNET TODAY

E-commerce is expected to reach $40 billion, and online business is anticipated to increase by 500 percent through 2010. Your business needs guidance from today's successful Internet marketing veterans. Learn the most efficient ways to bring consumers to your site, get visitors to purchase, how to up-sell, oversights to avoid, and how to steer clear of years of disappointment.

We spent countless hours interviewing hundreds of today's most successful e-commerce marketers. This book not only chronicles their achievements, but is a compilation of their secrets and proven successful ideas. It has hundreds of hints, tricks, and secrets on how to make money (or more money) with your Web site.

There are many book sand courses on Internet marketing; this is the only book that will provide you with insider secrets. With real-life examples of how successful businesses market their products online, the information is so useful that you can read a page and put the idea into action.

ISBN-13: 978-0-910627-65-8
288 Pages • $21.95

To order call 1-800-814-1132 or visit www.atlantic-pub.com

Internet marketing revealed Methods:
The complete guide to becoming an internet marketing expert

Internet Marketing Revealed is a carefully tested, well-crafted, and complete tutorial on a subject vital to Web developers and marketers. This book teaches the fundamentals of online marketing implementation, including Internet strategy planning, the secrets of search engine optimization (SEO), successful techniques to be first in Google and Yahoo!, vertical portals, effective online advertisement, and innovative e-commerce development. This book will help you understand the e-business revolution as it provides strong evidence and practical direction in a friendly and easy-to-use self-study guide.

Respected author and educator Miguel Todaro has created a complete introduction to Internet marketing that is instructive, clear, and insightful. This book is the result of several years of research and deep professional experience implementing online solutions for major corporations. Written in an instructive way, you will find fundamental concepts explained along with detailed diagrams. Many short examples illustrate just one or two concepts at a time, encouraging you to master new topics by immediately putting them to use.

ISBN-13: 978-1-60138-265-8
288 Pages • $24.95

THE COMPLETE GUIDE TO WRITING WEB-BASED ADVERTISING COPY TO GET THE SALE: WHAT YOU NEED TO KNOW EXPLAINED SIMPLY

Since the advent of the Internet and since more and more people are making purchases online, writers have had to adapt to composing copy for the Web. Contrary to what many people think, writing for the Web and writing for print are not the same and involve very different skill sets. Instead of struggling to find the right words, copywriters should read this new book from cover to cover to discover how to write sales-generating copy.

The Complete Guide to Writing Web-based Advertising Copy to Get the Sale will teach you how to make your copy readable and compelling, how to reach your target audience, how to structure the copy, how to visually format the copy, how to forget everything you ever learned about writing, how to pull in visitors, how to convince visitors to buy, how to outline and achieve your goals, how to create a customer profile, how to create a unique selling position, how to include searchable keywords in the copy, how to convert prospects to paying customers, and how to compose eye-catching headlines.

ISBN-13: 978-1-60138-232-0
288 Pages • $24.95

To order call 1-800-814-1132 or visit www.atlantic-pub.com

DID YOU BORROW THIS COPY?

Have you been borrowing a copy of *Word-of-Mouth Advertising Online and Off: How to Spark Buzz, Excitement, and Free Publicity for Your Business or Organization - With Little or No Money* from a friend, colleague, or library? Wouldn't you like your own copy for quick and easy reference? To order, photocopy the form below and send to:

Atlantic Publishing Company
1405 SW 6th Ave • Ocala, FL 34471-0640